Reginald Wood

FINALLY
A FACE

Published by Mischief Makers
17 Norfolk Road, Tunbridge Wells, Kent, TN1 1TD.

British Library Cataloguing in Publication Data.
A catalogue record for this volume is available from the British Library.

ISBN 978-0-9555433-9-5

Photos: Reginald Wood (this page)
Front Cover: Charterhouse School cricket team 1876

Printed and bound by Catford Print Centre (020 8695 0101)

Introduction

We live in an era when we have full career records, photographs and biographical trivia of all of those who have played Test cricket recently for England and even records of those in the embryonic days of Test cricket are virtually complete following dedicated research by the game's band of enthusiasts, historians and researchers.

There are plenty of tour group photographs that have captured virtually every player lucky enough to be selected by England. Even Basil Grieve, whose grave I found in Eastbourne in the summer of 2005 and who played just two first-class matches (both Tests in South Africa in March 1889), has been captured on film.

This book came about after I decided to prioritise a hobby of tracing cricketers' graves and dedicate more time to locating those who had been capped by England. It was recorded that Wood died in Manly, Sydney, Australia, so I sent an e-mail to the local council which in turn was passed on. John MacRitchie, the Local Studies Librarian at Manly Library, quickly replied and stated that Wood was buried in Manly Cemetery, although his final resting place was not marked with a headstone. He was also able to add some more details to those already known about Wood and also forwarded a brochure relating to the cemetery which highlighted others who had achieved fame in a variety of ways and who were interred within its walls. Yet Wood had been overlooked and until the e-mail arrived they were unaware of the Test player in their midst.

Although initially elated to have located him, any possibility that I was the first to have done so for many years dissolved on finding an article by R.L. Arrowsmith in *The Cricketer* magazine dated May 14th 1960 which mentioned Wood's burial location and gave a decent review of his short career. It mentioned that "more than one enquiry has appeared in *The Cricketer* at some time for the whereabouts or date of death of Reginald Wood". The author also gives thanks to a Mr E. A. Malaher, the Honorary Treasurer of the Old Carthusian Club, whose "indefatigable research" had assisted him in this quest.

I mentioned Wood to a few of the game's historians and writers and one informed me that he was England's only Test player of whom there is no known photograph, a story which was found to be repeated on the Internet.

Although a member of the "One Cap Club" his details are reasonably well documented. He was born in 1860 and it has been noted in cricket books that he attended Charterhouse School in Godalming, Surrey. That he was the only player not represented on film should surely have driven the journalists of generations of years gone by to follow the path of cricket researcher Mike Spurrier, well known for his erudite work on those players "killed in action", who often contacted their schools and from these institutions obtained a wealth of information and often photographs to accompany his own in-depth research.

Roger Packham contacted me to say that he had a carte de visite of the 1876 Charterhouse cricket team and that Wood was listed on the back. However there was no indication of which one of the eleven young men was him. I then e-mailed the school to enquire if they had a copy of the 1876 team photograph and soon received a reply confirming that they had a copy of the one in Roger's possession, and also a much larger copy which <u>did</u> name the players in the correct order. They kindly sent me a copy of the latter.

So, in October 2005 I took possession of an excellent photocopy of the said photograph which had lain in the archives of Charterhouse School for nearly 130 years, the game's historians sadly unaware of its existence.

I offered the story to *The Manchester Evening News* who failed to reply to my e-mail and to *The Sunday Telegraph,* who did but then decided to overlook it. More research was done by the archivist at the school and then I decided to write a brief biography, or perhaps it should be seen as an extended essay of a man whom photography appeared to have overlooked.

Despite the amount of research done, much is missing about his life, so a proper biography will, I feel, never be able to be completed as he appears to have disappeared from public life soon after playing his last first-class match in Australia. There are a few snippets about him tucked away in cricket books and magazines and also on the Internet, so this book attempts to pool together all of these facts and figures, information that I have been sent and details that I have found. It also contains a lot of statistics and information gleaned at the British Library Newspaper Library in Colindale, London taken from *The Birkenhead News and Wirral Advertiser* newspaper. However, despite much success, fate turned its hand as, although the library has copies of the newspaper back to 1878, that particular year and those up to 1881 inclusive are too fragile to be handled. It must also be remembered that Wood may have made his debut for the Birkenhead club as early as 1876. At some stage in the future it is intended to transfer these fragile copies onto microfilm and that may in turn reveal more details about Wood as a teenager.

His birthplace of Birkenhead is documented, as is his death in Sydney, but it is unclear why he came so far south to Godalming, Surrey for an education and also why he stayed for only two years at the school. Also unfathomed is the exact reason for his emigration to Australia, although I did establish a reasonably accurate date when he left. And lastly, did he die with none of his relatives knowing that he had passed on?

On the other hand some previously unknown facts did come to light. Perhaps surprisingly, the fact that his mother hailed from Canada can be found on one cricket web-site on the Internet and as this fact is not entered on his birth certificate, clearly some research on him has been done in the past.

However, there are large chunks of his life which are still missing and it is clear that he travelled widely in Australia as we have addresses and jobs for him in Melbourne and Queensland prior to his death in Sydney. Alan Gill, an Old Carthusian and ex-journalist in Australia, kindly offered to check the old newspaper indices in both Melbourne and Sydney for any mention of our subject, but it appears that Wood managed to avoid their newspapers as well following his disappearance or retirement from playing in that country. Sadly we were therefore unable to fill in much of his life history and perhaps the details of his time in Australia will never be known, thus we must concede defeat on this issue and accept that his character and traits, likes and dislikes will not feature in this book.

Author Thomas Hardy once professed something along the lines of "if you are going to stop a man on his way down the street, make sure that you have something worth telling him." I hope that we have found enough in this book to make its purchase worthwhile and that it proves to be a valuable addition to cricket's historical books. Without the help, facts and figures gleaned by those on the acknowledgements page we would not have bothered stopping anyone as we would not have had enough to tell them and the book would also not have been written.

So, for the first time Wood's photograph graces a cricket publication (he is the young man second from the left in the middle row) and the myth that there is no photograph of him can be put to bed forever. There are now no England Test players lacking a photograph.

Philip Paine   June 2007

This is number 79 of 500 signed copies.

A Special Acknowledgement

On subsequent pages I have listed those whose assistance helped to bring this book to fruition. Each one added a vital piece of information which I would not have found myself and they allowed me to illustrate a part of Wood's life much more thoroughly.

I would however like to put on record a special note of thanks to **Roger Packham** who initially brought to my attention that there may be a photograph of Wood in existence. This ignited my enthusiasm and sent me on a quest to establish whether this was the case or not. Had his photograph not been located then this book would never have been considered and thus he would have remained perhaps England's most unknown cricketer. Little did I know, even when I took hold of the photograph, what further research lay ahead and where I would have to travel to glean further information about this most remote individual.

The twelve months of research was very rewarding, although the train journeys to libraries and Charterhouse School and hours sat typing up my findings were often tiring. I conducted more research when I was in Australia in December 2006 and January 2007 so the book has a global input. Information came to me by old routes: school magazines and new ones: the Internet.

Roger was then kind enough to offer me help with regard to the lay-out of the book, and corrected a few errors too, and for this extra assistance I am further grateful.

Acknowledgements

Don Ambrose and the "**Cricket Archive**" web-site
for supplying family and employment details.

R.L. Arrowsmith
whose article on Wood in "The Cricketer" added much to this book.

Charterhouse School
for allowing so much of their material to be published.

John Daniels
for sending on a copy of Wood's death certificate.

Chris Elston
for sending a second photograph of Wood, compiling career details and for taking
me to Birkenhead Park C.C. and to two of his homes.

David Frith
for sending a photograph of the 1887 Non-Smokers and Smokers teams and for
his correcting, encouragement and overseeing of this venture.

Alan Gill
for checking journalistic records in Australia.

Graham Goldsmith
for drafting up such a detailed family tree.

Peter Greville
for seeking out details of Wood's rugby career.

Manly Library
for allowing publication of the view of Manly from Kangaroo Hill dated c1915.

Margaret Mardall and Ann Wheeler
for their research into Wood's relatives, school studies and school match reports.

Greg McKie
whose article on Wood in the A.C.S. Journal number 74 added much to this book.

John MacRitchie
for passing on a map showing Wood's plot, details of other notables in Manly
Cemetery and for locating the 1915 Manly area photograph.

Philip Thorn
for passing on details of Wood's employment in 1911.

Warwick Torrens
for his research amongst his Queensland cricket records.

Chapters

Family Composition

The fact that very little is known about our subject is well documented and for any unknowing soul who may have set out to find out about him this fact would soon have become apparent.

It quickly became clear that others had been inclined to do some research on this most elusive of cricketers, but, like those before, had found very little. It does not help either that he was born with a reasonably common surname. So I feared that finding his birth certificate would be the first of many stiff challenges to overcome in attempting to compile a book of some sort about a player whom history seems to have embraced only quickly before losing him. Yet thankfully it transpired that he was the only Reginald Wood born in that era so his certificate was found in Volume 8a on page 399 in the birth register for June 1860.

At this early stage it should be noted that he is shown on his birth certificate as Reginald Wood. Yet when the photograph of him in the 1876 Charterhouse cricket team surfaced, on the front he is shown as "R. Wood" yet on the back of the smaller carte de visite version he is printed in as "A.R. Wood". No other person with that surname played for the school eleven that season

He was born on March 7th 1860, the sixth son and the tenth child of twelve from the marriage of John and Elizabeth Wood (nee Torrance). His father was born in Rochdale, Lancashire in 1808 yet John's sister (and Reginald's aunt) Martha was born in Islington, London in 1816. Come the 1851 census, she is shown residing in Priory Street, Birkenhead, an area where she remained for the rest of her life, as on the 1891 census she is shown as an unmarried seventy-five-year-old living in Oxton, Cheshire. Each census shows her living at a different address but always as unmarried and in the general area.

On the 1851 census Reginald's father John is listed as an American cotton merchant, aged 43 and living in Priory Street, Birkenhead with wife Elizabeth, although sadly there are no more details for the address, just the street name. Unfortunately his family name is very common and on checking the marriage registers for the relevant period it was not possible to establish when his parents married. Perhaps his wife's details give a clue as to why the date of their marriage cannot be established as she was born in Montreal, Canada in 1822. Indeed almost certain proof that they were married abroad, either in her native Canada or perhaps in America due to his trade came when Elizabeth's maiden name was established from Reginald's birth certificate. Despite further checks of the marriage registers for this period in order to look for her surname, which even then was probably rarer than Wood, they again revealed "no trace". Despite these missing details we can see that John married a lady fourteen years his junior and their first child, Elizabeth Torrance Wood, was christened on November 20th 1842 in Birkenhead.

Thus it can be seen that in common with many other females of the era, she married young and in her case took the brave decision to emigrate.

The 1861 census shows John and Elizabeth residing in Kirby, Cheshire, although again a fuller address is not given. John is shown as a merchant and his wife, abruptly, as such. It should be noted that they had five servants living with them at this time, all from West Kirby, and employed a cook, housemaid, laundress, nurse and under nurse to assist with the running of a household of at least twelve. At this time Reginald had just been born and his mother Elizabeth was part way through a five-year break between the birth of her tenth and eleventh children. The 1871 census shows John as a 63-year-old cotton merchant and Elizabeth as a 49-year-old wife, living at 3 Caroline Place, Birkenhead, Cheshire.

The 1881 census shows John employed as a merchant and Elizabeth again as a wife, and their address is given as 5 Slatey Road, Birkenhead, Cheshire. This was the last census in which John featured as he died in Birkenhead in 1887, aged 79. Elizabeth appears on the 1891 census as "widow, aged 69, living on own means" at 7 Kingsmead Road, Oxton, Cheshire. Perhaps she lived on some sort of pension or income following her husband's apparently successful career as a trader until her death aged 73, about June 1895 in Birkenhead. Despite checking various Cheshire local government databases for copies of John's or Elizabeth's wills it was not possible to find either.

A number of Reginald's brothers and sisters are missing from the censuses in the latter part of the 19th century – perhaps they moved abroad as one of their descendants married and had children in America? The twelve are listed on the following two pages, although the vagueness of their dates of birth is because their details were taken from the four quarterly birth registers each year. To get an exact date of birth a copy of the certificate would have to be ordered from the respective volumes:

Elizabeth Torrance Wood was born about 1842 in Birkenhead, Cheshire and was christened on November 20th 1842 in Birkenhead, Cheshire.

- She appeared as aged 58, unmarried on the census in 1901 in 70 Park Road West, Tranmere, Cheshire.

Charles Francis Wood was born about 1844 in Birkenhead, Cheshire.

- He appeared as merchant's apprentice, aged 17 on the census in 1861 in West Kirby, Cheshire.
- He appeared as general labourer, aged 57, single on the census in 1901 in Tranmere Union Workhouse, Birkenhead, Cheshire.

James Torrance Wood was born about March 1846 in Birkenhead, Cheshire.

Amy Gordon Wood was born about December 1848 in Birkenhead, Cheshire.

Ernest Reuss Wood was born on September 20th 1850 in Birkenhead, Cheshire.

- He appeared as retired cotton merchant, aged 50, single on the census in 1901 at 70 Park Road West, Tranmere, Cheshire.

He died March 31st 1907.

Jessie Theresa Wood was born about September 1852 in Tranmere, Cheshire.

- She appeared as Visitor, aged 18, unmarried on the census in 1871 in Tollemache Road, Claughton with Grange, Cheshire visiting sister Amy and married about March 1877 in Birkenhead, Cheshire.

John Torrance Wood was born about September 1854 in Tranmere, Cheshire.

Kate Vanneck Wood was born about 1857 in Tranmere, Cheshire and died on February 24th 1889 and is buried in Flaybrick Hill Cemetery.

Herbert Kennedy Wood was born on April 27th 1858 in West Kirby, Cheshire.

He died at Charterhouse School on April 7th 1874

Reginald Wood was born on March 7th 1860 in West Kirby, Cheshire.

- He appeared as aged 1 on the census in 1861 in West Kirby, Cheshire.
- He appeared as scholar, aged 11 on the census in 1871 at 3 Caroline Place, Birkenhead, Cheshire.
- He appeared as aged 21, unmarried on the census in 1881 at 5 Slatey Road, Birkenhead, Cheshire.

Frederick W. Wood was born about 1865 in West Kirby, Cheshire.

- He appeared as insurance clerk, aged 26 unmarried on the census in 1891 at 7 Kingsmead Road, Oxton, Cheshire.
- He appeared as insurance manager, aged 36, single on the census in 1901 at 70 Park Road West, Tranmere, Cheshire.

Alexander Galt Wood was born about December 1866 in West Kirby, Cheshire.

- He appeared as cotton salesman, aged 24 unmarried on the census in 1891 at 7 Kingsmead Road, Oxton, Cheshire.

As mentioned earlier, Reginald was the tenth of twelve children. The first was born in 1842 to a mother aged just 20, and the rest followed at intervals of roughly two years, the last one being born when she was 44 years old. Reginald was born when his mother was 38 and his father 52.

3 Caroline Place, Birkenhead

This photograph shows the huge and impressive house where he was living with his family at the time of the 1871 census. Although now divided into flats it has four floors, deep windows and a wide and impressive main entrance. It is located in a small and very select road, very close to his next home in Slatey Road and both are close to Birkenhead Park.

5 Slatey Road, Birkenhead

By the time of the 1881 census Reginald Wood was living at this smaller house, although by now his father was 73 and probably a few of his older siblings had left home too. It is a solid and impressive Victorian dwelling and no doubt very similar in appearance to when Reg lived there. The only downside is that the road carries a fair bit of passing traffic.

CERTIFIED COPY OF AN ENTRY OF BIRTH

GIVEN AT THE GENERAL REGISTER OFFICE

Application Number PAS 6042368

REGISTRATION DISTRICT   Wirral

1860. BIRTH in the Sub-district of Woodchurch   in the   County of Chester

Columns:-	1	2	3	4	5	6	7	8	9	10
No.	When and where born	Name, if any	Sex	Name and surname of father	Name, surname and maiden surname of mother	Occupation of father	Signature, description and residence of informant	When registered	Signature of registrar	Name entered after registration
143	Seventh March 1860 West Kirby	Reginald	Boy	John Ward	Elizabeth Fisher Ward formerly Torrance	Cotton Merchant	John Ward Father West Kirby	Seventh April 1860	Thomas Oliver Registrar	

CERTIFIED to be a true copy of an entry in the certified copy of a Register of Births in the District above mentioned.

Given at the GENERAL REGISTER OFFICE, under the Seal of the said Office, the   13th   day of   January   2006.

BXCB 442577

SPR

039887 10/07 08/05 SPSL 012032

Charterhouse School

The backdrop to this photograph is a view that would have been recognisable to Reginald. I took the shot on July 10th 2006 when I took the opportunity to visit the school to look for any more records of him in their archives and also to watch the Surrey second eleven play Kent's seconds in a one-day match. Five months later, and on the other side of the world, I was standing over his grave.

Schooldays

No information about Reginald Wood's junior school years has come to light yet. Despite being born and bred in Cheshire he joined Charterhouse School in Godalming, Surrey at the beginning of the Oration Quarter (autumn term) in 1874 and left at the end of the Cricket Quarter (summer term) in 1876. Thus his stay was brief. Whilst there he was in Lockites boarding house, named after Mr Lock, whose house he was in. School records list the boys in order of seniority – according to which form they were in – and although he was new to the school he had been placed in a form which was at the time relatively high up in the school. His name appears above some others who had joined the school earlier.

Two of his elder brothers also attended the school: Ernest, who joined in January 1865 and left in 1866 and who was in Verites house, and Herbert, who entered Lockites in Oration Quarter (autumn) 1873. The former went on to become a cotton trader in Liverpool and died March 31st 1907, but the latter died at the school on April 7th 1874.

The school was founded by Thomas Sutton in 1611 and its original home in London was on the site of a Carthusian monastery. It moved to its current site, a huge collection of purpose-built Gothic buildings designed by architect P.C. Hardwick, in 1872. The school has had many famous pupils throughout its rich history, including such luminaries as cricketers Peter May and Aubrey Smith, Queen Victoria's grandson, Prince Albert, Boy Scout founder Baden-Powell, composer Ralph Vaughan Williams, preacher John Wesley, playwright Ben Travers and mountaineers George Mallory, who died on Everest in 1924, and Wilfrid Noyce, who was part of the team that conquered it in 1953. It was not only individual pupils who went on to fame, as the Old Carthusian football team won the F.A. Cup in 1881 and a plaque below the flagpole which overlooks the main cricket pitch commemorates this achievement.

In 1875 Wood was in the under IVth form in class three (of four) and he studied Classics (Latin and Greek), French, Mathematics and Natural Science. In a class of 42 he finished 38th, 7th and 32nd respectively and by the following year he had moved up to the upper IVth form. He played cricket for the school in both years and also football, and reports for these matches still survive, though none of his academic reports survived. There appears to have been a good number of pupils from the north studying at the school and Mrs Wheeler, the school archivist, suggests that at the time "boarding was considered to confer great educational benefits and Charterhouse had a good reputation. The location of the school close to the railway also made it quite feasible for those who lived a long distance away". It is not clear however whether he was sent there because of his academic ability or purely to get a decent education. Whatever the reason for his attendance as the sixth son of a large family, he arrived at the school when aged fourteen and left aged sixteen.

He played for the school's cricket eleven and in 1876 took 95 wickets at 7.1. *Wisden* described his bowling as "extraordinary left-hand bowling – good action clean head work and effective alteration of pace".

Lillywhite meanwhile described him as "an extremely scientific and hard-working left-arm bowler". In 1876 whilst playing against M.C.C. and Ground he took 4-8 and against Westminster School he took 4-33 and 7-8 and also managed 38 runs. He was rated as "a useful left-handed batsman who hit the ball hard and freely". Greg McKie in an article on him noted that "Coming from an affluent background, it was surprising that he dropped out of school at the end of the year". School records for 1876 again show him in class three and again studying Classics, French and Natural Science, and in a class of 37 he finished 26th, 11th and 28th respectively, although perhaps his achievements in the Gallic language should be measured against the fact that his mother hailed from Montreal, a French-speaking city in Canada.

On the following pages are cricket match reports copied from *The Carthusian*, the school magazine which reports on many of the matches in which Wood played along with other different sports reports. As can be seen, the batting and bowling details are very well laid out and the reports vary between a brief resume of the respective fixture and a detailed account. There are many such reports available for his time at the school, so what follows is just a small selection to illuminate this excellent source of the school's sports history. He appears only to be mentioned in two other sports reports however, both football matches. One relates to a match on Saturday, January 29th 1876 when he played for Dark against Light, which his team won 3-2, and the other occurred on Wednesday February 23rd when he played for Town against Country which saw the latter win 4-0.

CHARTERHOUSE.

Subjects of the Classical Examination of the Lower School.

REMOVE.

Divinity: Acts of the Apostles. Greek Testament: the Gospel according to St. John.

Cicero: Pro Archiâ. Virgil: Georg. IV.

Herodotus: VI. 125—130 (inclusive); VII. 198—228 (inclusive). Euripides: Hecuba, 786 to end.

History: English: Houses of York and Lancaster. Greek: Smith's Greece, XVIII.—XXIV. (inclusive).

English: Shakespeare, Macbeth.

Repetition: Virgil: Georg. IV. 1—200. Cicero: Pro Archiâ, Chap. I., II., and VI.

UPPER IV. FORM.

Divinity: Acts of the Apostles. Greek Testament: St. John, Chap. I.—XII.

Horace: Odes II. Cicero in Catilinam, Chap. III.

Homer: Iliad VI. Xenophon: Anabasis, Lib. VI. Chap. 1—4.

History: English: House of Plantagenet. Roman: Samnite Wars.

Geography: Asia.

Vivâ-voce: Virgil: Georg. IV. 1—250.

Repetition: Horace, Odes II. 1—12.

UNDER IV. FORM.

Divinity: Acts of the Apostles. Greek Testament: Epistle to Hebrews, Chap. I.—VI. (inclusive).

Horace: Odes IV. and Carmen Seculare. Cicero: in Catilinam I.

Homer: Iliad III. Xenophon: Anabasis, Lib. VI. Chap. 1—3 (inclusive).

History: First and Second Punic Wars.

Geography: Great Britain, France, Spain and Portugal.

Repetition: Horace, Odes IV. 1—5 (inclusive).

Charterhouse Exam Results 1875

	Classical Order.	French.	Natural Science.
UNDER IV. FORM (*Continued*).			
CLASS II.			
Dyne, W. T.	3	24	17
Powell, E. O.	13	4	34
Trollope, A. H....	14	6	11
Hampson, G. F.	17	33	2
Norris, E. J.	15	8	41
Stantial, A. E....	20	23	24
Griffith, J. W.	16	22	36
Simpson, J. M....	21	20	13
Evelyn, W. A.	18	32	37
Taylor, T. L.	23	28	38
Haines, H. J.	22	18	19
Borthwick, J. A.	28	37	6
Druce, G. C.	25	13	33
Warre, B. D.	29	11	25
Winckworth, H. G.	24	31	21
Bishop, F. W. F.	30	25	26
CLASS III.			
Loveless, C. J....	27	27	22
Stuart, A....	26	30	31
Cathcart, Hon. C	31	35	15
Evan-Thomas, O. G.	33	10	35
Tennant, C. C....	32	34	42
Archdale, W. F.	35	19	16
Hansell, R. G.	36	26	20
Wood, R.	38	7	32
King, A.	34	38	23

Above are listed some of the school exam results for Classical Order, French and Natural Science. Wood was in Class Three of the "Under Fourth Form" and whilst he finishes towards the top in French, his ability in the other two subjects is clearly not as good.

LIGHT v. DARK.

This game was begun on June 23rd, and ended in a single innings victory for Dark. In the first innings of Light Abdy and White both played well, making up the greater part of the score between them. In this innings Jeaffreson took four wickets for seven runs. Light were unfortunately deficient in bowling, being deprived of Dobbie's services, or otherwise the victory might not have been so decided. Hulton hit very freely for his 61, which is one of the highest scores of the season. In the second innings Jeaffreson's bowling proved most deadly, taking 10 wickets for 18 runs; the whole score being 36.

LIGHT.

A. J. Wake, b Ainslie	1	c and b Jeaffreson		5
E. F. White, b Ainslie	38	b Jeaffreson		1
N. J. Abdy, b Ainslie	30	b Jeaffreson		3
E. F. Growse, b Jeaffreson	10	b Jeaffreson		1
C. T. Winney, b Carter	0	b Jeaffreson		10
H. B. Southwell, b Jeaffreson	4	b Jeaffreson		7
E. C Wynyard, b Jeaffreson	7	b Jeaffreson		1
O. Evan Thomas, c Hayter, b Jeaffreson	5	b Jeaffreson		0
R. Wood. c Hayter, b Ainslie	0	b Jeaffreson		1
C. Pearson, c Burrows, b Ainslie	0	b Jeaffreson		0
G. Searle, not out	0	not out		0
Byes 1, l byes 1, wides 2	4	Byes 3, l byes 2, wides 2		7
	99			**36**

DARK.

L. Colebrooke, c Growse b Abdy	20	W. B. T. Hayter, b Thomas	11
A. Wilson, b Growse	0	C. A. Lovegrove, c and b Wood	8
H. G. Jeaffreson b Growse	3	E. M. Short, b Growse	3
C. L. N. Bishop, b Growse	0	H. Davidson, not out	0
G. C. Carter, Esq., b Growse	11	Byes 13, l byes 1, wides 2	16
G. H. Ainslie, b Growse	12		
R. E. Hulton, c Wood, b Thomas	61		**145**

2ND ELEVEN V. OLD CARTHUSIANS.

In the 2nd Eleven match we were more fortunate. In the first innings the Old Carthusians were got out for 65, of which various substitutes made a great proportion. The 2nd Eleven then went in and made 67, of which Wood made 15 in very good style. In the next innings the Old Carthusians were fully represented and made 93; and the 2nd Eleven made the 92, which they required to win, with the loss of six wickets. Reeve played well for his 30 not out. Score:

OLD CARTHUSIANS.

1st Innings.		2nd Innings.	
T. J. Atherton b Stokes... ...	2	c Reeve b E. Thomas ...	0
E. Williams b E. Thomas ...	7	b Stokes	12
W. C. Williams b E. Thomas .	2	st Southwell b E Thomas...	3
Rev. C. S. Gibson b Stokes ...	0	c Somers-Cocks b E. Thomas	11
Rev. O. S. Walford b E. Thomas	2	not out	1
C. G. Paget b Stokes	0	run out	3
E. A. Deakin b Stokes	12	c and b Stokes	39
Rev. E. L. Pearson b E. Thomas	16	b E. Thomas	0
J. Lant c Reeve b E. Thomas ...	21	b Stokes	14
H. D. Verelst run out	0	b E. Thomas	6
W. Empson (sub) not out ...	1	c Pearson b E. Thomas ...	0
Bye 1, l bye 1, ...	2	Byes 0, leg byes 3, wide 1...	4
	65		93

PRESENT CARTHUSIANS.

1st Innings.		2nd Innings.	
H. Whinney lbw b Atherton ...	0	lbw b Atherton	7
H. Somers-Cocks b Atherton ...	0	b Atherton	0
C. A. Lovegrove b Atherton ...	0	b Lant	1
H. B. Southwell b Atherton ...	7	b Atherton	
C. A. Reeve b Atherton ...	11	not out	
R. Wood b Atherton	15	c Paget b Atherton... ...	
E. Thomas c Lant b Atherton ..	12	c Gibson b Williams ...	12
E. Wynyard b Atherton... ...	1	not out	
C. Pearson b Lant	6		
A. Keightley b Atherton ...	1		
A. R. Stokes not out	0		
Byes 3. l bye 1, wides 9, no balls 1	14	Byes 9, l byes 3, wides 4	16
	67		92

Football.

This match was played on Wednesday, February 23rd. Tod kicked off soon after 2.30, and after a well contested game, the Country remained victors by four goals to none. Short was unfortunately hurt during the game, which undoubtedly contributed greatly to the victory of the Country. For the first half of the game the ball was kept well down by the Town's goal; and two goals were kicked by Wake and Tod respectively. After half-time two more goals were kicked, and Keightley made some good runs. For the Town, Hayter as back was most useful, while for Country, Wilson and Williams were conspicuous.

TOWN :—E. M. Short (capt.), C. Tancock, Esq., C. A. Reeve, R. S. S. Baden-Powell, W. T. B. Hayter (back), J. Eddis, B. Burrows, A. T. Davies, R. Wood, O. Evan-Thomas, C. C. Maingay (half back).

COUNTRY :—A. H. Tod (capt.), A. W. F. Wilson (half-back), C. J. Cornish, A. J. Wake, G. D. Keightley, E. F. Growse, A. C. Parry, H. Williams, A. Keightley, H. Randall, H. Devenish.

Football.

"Old Carthusians" will be played this year on Saturday, March 11th.

A match has been arranged with the Aldershot Division for Wednesday, March 15th.

LIGHT *v.* DARK.

Played on Saturday, January 29th. As soon as the ball was kicked off, Page began with some very pretty dribbling, but the ball was taken down again and a goal obtained for Dark by a fine kick from Williams. Abdy after a good run down sent the ball through the Dark goal, which was soon after again in jeopardy, but was saved by the exertions of A. Keightley. A run down by Cornish, and another by Hayter were both unsuccessful, and a beautiful run down by Reeve, who passed the backs very cleverly, failed through want of backing up. A splendid run down by Short was, however, more successful, and Reeve, after a good piece of play, middled the ball to G. D. Keightley, who kicked the third goal for Dark. Ten minutes before "all over" Page obtained another goal for Light by a good long shot, and on the ball being kicked off again, two fine squashes resulted from corner kicks just outside the Light goal, from which the ball had just been extricated, when "all over" was called. Thus, after a hard fought game, the Dark were victors by three goals to two. For Dark, Wilson (half-back) and Reeve played very well, while Abdy and Wake (half-back) did great service to Light.

LIGHT:—N. J. Abdy (capt.), W. R. Page, R. S. S. Baden-Powell (back), A. J. Wake (half-back), E. F. Growse, A. C. Parry, B. Burrows, H. Randall, A. T. Davies, O. Evan-Thomas, G. Swaine, C. Boscawen.

DARK :—E. M. Short (capt), A. W. Wilson (half-back), C. A. Reeve, C. J. Cornish, L. H. Burrows, G. D. Keightley, W. T. B. Hayter (back), H. Williams, A. Keightley, R. Wood, H. Devenish.

CHARTERHOUSE.

EXAMINATION 1876.

Subjects of the Classical Examination of the Under School.

REMOVE.

Divinity: St. Luke, with Greek Testament, Chap. XII.—XXIV.

Horace: Odes I. Cicero: Epistles (Clarendon Press Selection) I.—X.

Homer: Odyssey IX. 1—479.

History: Greek: Confederacy of Delos and Peloponnesian War. English: Reign of Henry VIII.

UPPER FOURTH FORM.

Divinity: St. Luke. Greek Testament: St. Luke, Chap. XIII.—XXIV.

Horace: Odes I. Cicero: Orat. in Cat. II. and III. §§ 1—6.

Homer: Iliad IX. 1—501. Xenophon: Anabasis VII. 6—8.

History: Greek: Peloponnesian War to 416 B.C. English: Henry VIII.

Geography: British Isles.

Repetition: Horace, Odes, I. 1—12.

UNDER FOURTH FORM.

Divinity: Genesis, Chap. I.—XXXIII. Greek Testament: Acts of the Apostles, Chap. I.—XII.

Horace: Odes IV. and Carmen Sæculare. Cicero: Orat. in Cat. I.

Homer: Iliad V. 1—500. Xenophon: Anabasis VII. 1—3.

History: Roman: 133—91 B.C. English: Norman Kings.

Geography: South America.

Repetition: Horace, Odes IV. 1—4.

Charterhouse Exam Results 1876

	Classical Order.	French.	Natural Science.
REMOVE (*Continued.*)			
CLASS III.			
Haworth, W. S., *French Prize*	27	1	29
Paget, C. E.	31	26	20
Gould, L. F.	21	33	34
Bishop, F. W. F.	33	18	28
Mildmay, W. H. St. J.	34	25	26
UPPER IV. FORM (A.)			
CLASS I.			
Story, W. H., *Mathematical Prize*	4	9	8
Sheppard, W. F.	10	31	2
Stavert, T. H., *Natural Science Prize*	15	2	1
Guillemard, L. N., *Classical Prize*	1	6	12
Holman, H. M.	2	7	4
CLASS III.			
Dumergue, H. W.	25	27	23
Page, H. M., *French Prize* ...	24	1	14
Tennant, C. C.	21	22	27
Cole, A. L.	29	15	5
Ponsonby, W. G.	23	10	32
Ainslie, G. H.	28	16	15
Hewett, R. M.	30	36	6
Wood, R.	26	11	28
Somers-Cocks, H. H.	27	32	34

A gain his ability with French is clear to see, but he has also made improvements in the other two subjects in what was to be his last year at the school.

FOOTBALL SEASON, 1875–6.

The result of this season is as follows :—

Matches played, 11 ; Won, 8 ; Lost, 3 ; Drawn, 0.

At an Eleven Meeting, held on Tuesday, March 14th, C. J. Cornish received his colours.

At an Eleven Meeting, held on Friday, March 24th, the following received their colours :—

A. J. Wake, W. T. B. Hayter, R. S. S. Baden-Powell, G. D. Keightley, L. H. Burrows.

THE ELEVEN.

*E. M. Short (Captain)—A fine dribbler, most useful as a forward, and as Captain always set a good example to the Eleven.

W. R. Page—A very neat dribbler and sticks well to the ball, rather selfish, was unfortunately absent the greater part of the season.

*A. H. Tod is of great use as a forward, and backs up well. Somewhat erratic in the proximity of goal.

*A. W. F. Wilson—A most useful half-back, being very firm on his legs, and kicking with great judgement. Rather excitable.

*C. A. Reeve—A fast forward, and of great service on the outside. Seldom kicks the ball out.

*C. J. Cornish—The fastest player in the Eleven, very energetic, and a good charger. Too much inclined to kick the ball out.

*A. J. Wake—A fair half-back, using his weight with great effect. Is also good as a forward.

W. T. B. Hayter—A safe back. Improved wonderfully towards the end of the season.

*R. S. S. Baden-Powell—A good goal-keeper, always keeping very cool.

G. D. Keightley—Very uncertain. Can dribble well when he likes.

*L. H. Burrows—A somewhat erratic player. Has been very unfortunate.

*N. J. Abdy was unable to play during the season, and therefore resigned the Captaincy, and has been made an honorary member of the Eleven.

* Leaving.

The Second, Third, and Fourth Elevens were filled up as follows :—

2ND ELEVEN :—E. F. Growse (capt.), H. Williams, J. Eddis, A. C. Parry, B. Burrows, H. Devenish, R. Wood, A. Keightley, H. Randall, G. W. Swaine, B. Boscawen.

3RD ELEVEN :—A. T. Davies (capt.), H. H. Dobbie, O. Evan-Thomas, L. Evan-Thomas, C. C. Maingay, J. Easton, L. Colebrooke, A. R. Stokes, E. M. Williams, R. W. Hewett, W. J. Smith.

4TH ELEVEN :—W. E. C. Frith, S. F. Smith, H. Davidson, J. F. M. Prinsep, C. Reid, H. Deare, A. King, H. Dickinson, H. Prance, H. R. Butler, W. Wynne.

Charterhouse Cricket Team 1876

Matches played 15
Won 13
Lost 2

E.G.Colvin E.F.Ainslie H.H.Dobbie W.T.B.Hayter E.F.Growse
A.F.Wilson R.Wood N.J.Aldy H.M.Davidson.
O.EvanThomas 1876 E.L.Colebrooke

This photograph is the one that has been in the possession of the school, probably since it was taken over 130 years ago. Unlike the carte de visite, it has their names inked in underneath below their respective positions. In this photograph he is referred to as R. Wood, and it can be seen that the eleven played 15 matches and won 13 and lost 2.

Carte de Visite

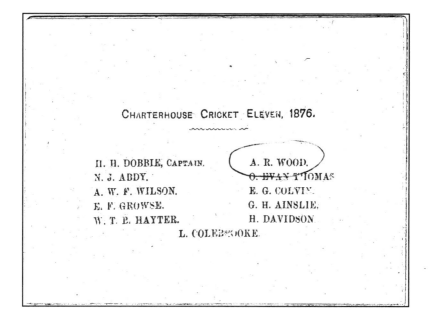

CHARTERHOUSE CRICKET ELEVEN, 1876.

II. H. DOBBIE, CAPTAIN.   A. R. WOOD.
N. J. ABDY.   O. EVAN T'IOMAS
A. W. F. WILSON.   E. G. COLVIN.
E. F. GROWSE.   G. H. AINSLIE,
W. T. P. HAYTER.   H. DAVIDSON.
          L. COLEBROOKE.

The rear of the carte de visite shows the subject listed as A.R. Wood. The team's names are listed in two vertical columns and not, as would have been more helpful, in three horizontal lines to assist with identification. No other Wood played for the school this season so there are no doubts that this is him. On the following pages are match reports for the 1876 season taken from *The Carthusian*, the Charterhouse School magazine. I have not re-typed them; in order give the book more of a feel of the era.

CHARTERHOUSE *v.* CHARTERHOUSE VAGABONDS.

This match was played on April 16th, and won by nine runs on the first innings. The Eleven played well, considering it was the first match of the season. Dobbie's bowling was very effective, and he also made his runs in the first innings in good style. Ainslie and Davidson made a good stand at the end of the second innings, the latter hitting very hard.

CHARTERHOUSE.

1st Innings.		2nd Innings.	
E. L. Colebrooke c and b Parry	2	c Romanis b Young... ...	0
A. J. Wake b Young	0	b Blomfield	1
N. J. Abdy b Young	14	c Blomfield	0
A. Wilson c Blomfield b Parry	7	b Blomfield	1
H. H. Dobbie b Young ...	16	b Blomfield	1
W. Hayter b Young	1	st Marshall b Young ...	5
H. S. Cocks b Parry	0	not out	8
G. H. Ainslie b Young... ...	8	c Romanis b Batten ...	19
G. Searle b Young	1	b Batten	1
A. Wood not out	3	b Young	0
R. Davidson c Marshall b Young	2	b Young	13
Bye 1	1	Byes 2, leg-bye 1 ...	3
	55		52

ANALYSIS OF THE BOWLING.

1st Innings.

	Balls.	Runs.	Mdn. Overs.	Wkts.	Wides.	No Balls.
G. Young, Esq.... ...	95	17	9	7	0	0
E. H. Parry, Esq. ...	90	37	3	3	0	0

2nd Innings.

	Balls.	Runs.	Mdn. Overs.	Wkts.	Wides.	No Balls.
E. G. Blomfield, Esq. ...	50	23	4	4	0	0
G. Young, Esq.... ...	55	20	3	4	0	0
J. M. Batten, Esq. ...	19	3	1	2	0	0
J. H. Merryweather, Esq.	10	3	0	0	0	0

CHARTERHOUSE VAGABONDS.

1st Innings.		2nd Innings.	
E. H. Parry, Esq., b Dobbie ...	0		
G. Young, Esq., run out ...	1		
E. G. Blomfield, Esq., b Ainslie	3	b Dobbie	21
J. M. Batten, Esq., b Ainslie ...	14	b Dobbie	0
Rev. W. Romanis b Dobbie ...	2	not out	11
M. Marshall, Esq., c Cocks b Ainslie	10	not out	8
F. Horner, Esq., b Dobbie ...	2		
G. C. Carter, Esq., b Dobbie ...	4		
J. H. Merryweather, Esq., b Dobbie	2		
T. P. Gandell, Esq., b Dobbie	0		
T. E. Page, Esq., not out ...	3		
Byes 3, wides 2	5	Byes 2	2
	46		42

ANALYSIS OF THE BOWLING.

1st Innings.

	Balls.	Runs.	Mdn. Overs.	Wkts.	Wides.	No Balls.
H. H. Dobbie	88	18	7	6	1	0
G. H. Ainslie	85	25	7	3	1	0

2nd Innings.

	Balls.	Runs.	Mdn. Overs.	Wkts.	Wides.	No Balls.
H. H. Dobbie	35	16	2	2	0	0
G. H. Ainslie	35	22	1	0	0	0

CHARTERHOUSE *v.* MR. A. C. EDDIS' ELEVEN.

This was the first match of the quarter, and resulted in a victory for us by four runs on the first innings. Colebrooke and Somers Cocks went to the wicket first for us. The latter was unfortunately run out, and followed by Abdy, who, together with Colebrooke, made the runs fast. The second wicket fell for 56 ; Dobbie followed, but was bowled by G. Young after he had made 7. Wilson then joined Abdy, who was bowled soon after also by G. Young, after a very good innings of 36, including one 6 and one 5. Four wickets down for 74. Hayter followed Abdy, and began to hit freely, when he was caught after making 11, the score standing at 96. Growse and Thomas made little resistance, the latter being run out. Ainslie then joined Wilson, who was soon after bowled by G. Young. Wood and Ainslie then raised the score to 131 before they were parted, and the last wicket added 12 more, making a total of 143. G. Young proved himself the most fatal of the bowlers, but not so much so as usual. The foreigners then went in, and began well, the first four wickets, with the exception of the second, all making over 20. Four wickets for 96. The next three added only 9 to the score. The eighth wicket did not fall until 127 had been made, and the last two wickets fell amidst great excitement for 132 and 139 respectively just before the stumps were drawn. Dobbie and Wood divided the honours of the bowling very equally and creditably.

CHARTERHOUSE.

E. L. Colebrooke c Fellowes b Eddis	20
H. Somers Cocks run out	3
N. J. Abdy b G. Young	36
H. H. Dobbie b G. Young	7
A. Wilson b G. Young	26
W. T. B. Hayter st Eddis b G. Young	11
E. F. Growse b G. Young	0
R. Wood c Shadwell b J. H. Young	19
G. H. Ainslie b J. H. Young	10
O. Evan-Thomas run out	0
H. Davidson not out	5
Byes 2, leg-bye 1, wides 3	6
	143

ANALYSIS OF THE BOWLING.

	Balls.	Runs.	Mdn. Overs.	Wkts.	Wides.
G. Young, Esq.	170	54	17	5	0
J. H. Young, Esq.	124	46	9	2	1
J. Wilkes, Esq.	10	16	0	0	2
A. Eddis, Esq.	35	21	1	1	0

MR. EDDIS' ELEVEN.

G. Young, Esq., c Growse b Dobbie	26
W. G. Fellowes, Esq., b Wood	5
J. Wilkes, Esq., b Wood	23
Rev. W. F. J. Romanis b Wood	24
J. D'd. Hartley, Esq., l-b-w b Wood	12
W. Eddis, Esq., b Dobbie	0
J. H. Young, Esq., b Wood	1
T. Pears, Esq., b Dobbie	12
L. L. Shadwell, Esq., c and b Dobbie	10
E. G. Colvin c Abdy b Dobbie	6
A. C. Eddis not out	1
Byes 14, leg-byes 4, wide 1	19
	139

ANALYSIS OF THE BOWLING.

	Balls.	Runs.	Mdn. Overs.	Wkts.	Wides
H. H. Dobbie	131	53	8	5	1
R. Wood	155	58	9	5	0
G. H. Ainslie	25	9	2	0	0

CHARTERHOUSE *v.* EXETER COLLEGE.

This match was played on Wednesday, June 14th, and resulted in a victory for us by 33 runs on the first innings. We went in first, and were represented by Colebrooke and Thomas. The first wicket fell when the score had reached 16, on the latter returning the ball to the bowler, H. Gibson. Dobbie then joined Colebrooke, and the two set to work scoring fast, until Dobbie was dismissed by a ball from Foord-Kelcey, after making 23, the telegraph standing at 57. Abdy followed, and Colebrooke continued to score fast, until Abdy was bowled by Horsman. Soon after this Colebrooke was caught by Foord-Kelcey, after a capital innings. Wilson, who had followed Abdy, was joined by Hayter, who was bowled by Latham in the same over, and then by Wood, who was unfortunately run out. Six wickets were down for 93, when Colvin joined Wilson, and stayed in until 27 had been added to the score, Wilson scoring fast. Growse began well, when he was dismissed by a capital catch at point by Horsman. Wilson was caught almost immediately after for a very free-hitting innings of 39. The last wicket fell in consequence of a clumsy piece of running when the total had reached 144. The Exeter Eleven then went in, and were represented by W. Foord-Kelcey and J. D. Horsman. Foord-Kelcey hit the first ball from Dobbie for 4, and was bowled by the next. H. Gibson followed, and he and Horsman ran the score up to 43 before the latter was bowled by Dobbie. The next three wickets fell to Dobbie in as many overs, until five wickets had fallen for 49. E. H. Parry and J. H. Forbes were then together, and raised the score to 58, when the latter was well caught by Ainslie, and was replaced by J. Bennett. Parry's was the next wicket to fall, being sharply stumped by Colvin when he appeared to be getting well into his work. F. Gresley joined Bennett, and the score had reached 92 when the latter was bowled by Ainslie. The last wickets added 19 to the score, bringing the total up to 111. In the second innings our wickets fell fast at first, until Dobbie and Wood got together. There was not, however, time to finish the match.

CHARTERHOUSE.

1st Innings.		2nd Innings.	
E. L. Colebrooke c Foord-Kelcey b Latham	44	c and b Benson	3
O. Evan-Thomas c and b Gibson	6		
N. J. Abdy b Horsman	4	b Benson	0
A. W. Wilson c Nevill b Gibson	39	b Gibson	1
H. H. Dobbie b Foord-Kelcey	23	not out	5
W. T. B. Hayter b Latham	0	c Horsman b Benson	0
R. Wood run out	0	not out	9
E. G. Colvin c Parry b Latham	9		
E. F. Growse c Horsman b Benson	5		
G. H. Ainslie b Benson	6		
H. Somers Cocks run out	1	b Benson	0
H. Davidson not out	0		
Byes 4, leg-bye 1, wides 2	7		
	144		18

ANALYSIS OF THE BOWLING—1st Innings.

	Balls.	Runs.	Mdn. Overs.	Wkts.	Wides.
H. Gibson, Esq.	75	23	6	2	0
E. H. Parry, Esq.	30	11	1	0	0
J. H. Forbes, Esq.	35	12	4	0	0
J. P. Benson, Esq.	40	21	2	2	1
W. Foord-Kelcey, Esq.	40	10	5	1	1
F. Gresley, Esq.	25	12	1	0	0
J. D. Horsman, Esq.	35	29	0	1	0
R. M. Latham, Esq.	40	21	1	3	0
2nd Innings.					
J. P. Benson, Esq.	30	7	2	4	0
H. Gibson, Esq.	25	12	2	1	0

EXETER COLLEGE.

W. Foord-Kelcey, Esq., b Dobbie		4
J. D. Horsman, Esq., c Hayter b Dobbie		8
H. Gibson, Esq., c and b Dobbie		20
J. S. Hewson, Esq., b Dobbie		1
J. P. Benson, Esq., c and b Dobbie		1
E. H. Parry, Esq., st Colvin b Wood		16
J. H. Forbes, Esq., c Ainslie b Wood		2
J. Bennett, Esq., b Ainslie		12
F. S. Gresley, Esq., b Dobbie		9
H. Nevill, Esq., b Growse		0
H. E. Hotham, Esq., c Growse b Ainslie		7
R. M. Latham, Esq., not out		0
Byes 29, leg-bye 1, wide 1		31
		111

ANALYSIS OF THE BOWLING.

	Balls.	Runs.	Mdn. Overs.	Wkts.	Wides.
H. H. Dobbie	126	43	7	6	0
R. Wood	105	28	10	2	1
G. Ainslie	35	1	6	2	0
E. F. Growse	15	7	1	1	0

OLD CARTHUSIANS.

Old Carthusians came off on June 29th. There were three Elevens which were all filled up. A great number of Old Carthusians came down from all parts, and the weather was most propitious. The Present Carthusians won all three matches. In the First Eleven match the Old Carthusians went in first, and made 98, of which the Rev. G. S. Davies' 16 and E. G. Blomfield's 32 were the best scores. The Present then went in, and the first wicket fell for 0, the second for 36, when Dobbie was caught after a good innings of 23, the third for 159. Thomas and Wilson brought the score up to this total, when Wilson was stumped after a very dashing and somewhat lucky innings of 71. Thomas was soon after caught by Drew, after making 58 in exceedingly good style. He played carefully and very well, and gave but one chance at the wicket during his innings. Abdy contributed 52 by some splendid hitting, including two sixes and two fives. The rest of the Eleven did not make many runs, and the total score was 230. W. C. Williams' bowling was very successful, and H. G. Jeaffreson's fielding was remarkably good. In the second innings of the Old Carthusians eight wickets had fallen for 80 runs when the stumps were drawn. The most noticeable piece of fielding in this innings was a capital catch by Growse at point. Dobbie and Wood divided the wickets in both innings. In the Second Eleven match the Present won by an innings and 80 runs to spare. In this game Somers Cocks played a capital innings of 73. In the Third Eleven match the Present won by eight wickets. The full scores will be given in our next number. A large number of visitors appeared in the course of the afternoon, and with these and the Old Carthusians, who mustered in great force, Green was very full, and the day a very successful one.

CHARTERHOUSE v. ESHER.

This match was played on June 21st, and resulted in a victory for us by 14 runs on the first innings. We went in first, and were represented by Colebrooke and Thomas, to the bowling of C. C. Clarke and Bristow. Thomas was caught off Clarke in the sixth over, and followed by Dobbie, who again was bowled by Clarke after four overs. Abdy then joined Colebrooke, but the latter was bowled in the same over by Clarke, and the next two overs disposed of Abdy and Wilson, while Hayter lasted through one more, and then succumbed to a ball from Clarke. Six wickets had now fallen for 38 runs, when Colvin joined Wood at the wicket, and these two brought the score up to 69 before Wood was bowled by Clarke. Colvin was bowled by Bristow when the score was at 82, and, when Growse was caught, the ninth wicket fell for 86. Ainslie and Davidson then made a stand, and brought the score up to 104, when the former was caught. W. S. Hodgson and Bristow then went in for the Esher Eleven, to the bowling of Dobbie and Wood. Wood bowled Bristow in his first, and F. Richards who followed him, in his third over. In the next over, C. C. Clarke was bowled by Dobbie, and G. Bird was caught by Hayter in Dobbie's next over. Four wickets had thus fallen for 21 runs before luncheon. Soon after luncheon Hodgson was caught by Wilson off Wood, and M. Marshall joined C. H. Clark. Runs were put together fast, and the telegraph shewed 84 for six wickets, when Marshall was bowled by Wood for a hard-hitting innings of 16. In the next over Wood also bowled Clark, after a good innings of 34, including one 7, and the last three wickets fell very quickly. As will be seen by the analysis, both Dobbie and Wood bowled capitally. In the second innings Dobbie played well for his 26, which was remarkable for the absence of singles, as it included one 5, one 4, five 3's, and one 2. On the whole, the batting of the Eleven was not so good as it has been this season, but the bowling and fielding were quite up to the average. Score :—

CHARTERHOUSE.

	1st Innings.		2nd Innings.	
E. L. Colebrooke b Clarke	... 11	c Hodgson b Bird ...	... 17
O. Evan-Thomas c Richards b Clark	... 3	c Marshall b Clarke...	... 5
H. H. Dobbie b Clarke	... 4	c Hickson b Clarke ...	... 26
N. J. Abdy b Bristow ...	... 7	c Hodgson b Bird ...	... 5
A. Wilson b Clarke ...	... 0	b Clarke ...	... 4
W. T. B. Hayter b Clarke	... 5	c Clarke b Bird	... 0
R. Wood b Clarke ...	... 25	c Richards b Bird ...	... 0
E. G. Colvin b Bristow	... 19	c and b Bird...	... 0
E. F. Growse c Clark b Clarke	... 4	c and b Clarke	... 8
G. H. Ainslie c McDonald b Clarke	... 12	not out ...	... 1
H. Davidson not out ...	... 9	h-w b Clarke...	... 3
Byes 2, wides 2, leg-bye 1 ...	5	Byes ...	... 2
	104		71

ANALYSIS OF THE BOWLING.

1st Innings.	Balls.	Runs.	Mdn. Overs.	Wkts.	Wides
Bristow	90	36	5	2	0
C. C. Clarke, Esq.	83	48	2	7	1
M. Hickson, Esq.	15	10	0	0	1
C. H. Clark, Esq.	10	3	1	1	0
2nd Innings.					
C. C. Clarke, Esq.	44	36	0	5	0
G. Bird, Esq.	40	33	0	5	0

ESHER.

	1st Innings.		2nd Innings.		
W. S. Hodgson, Esq., c Wilson b Wood	15			
Bristow b Wood	5			
F. Richards, Esq., b Wood ...	3			
C. C. Clarke, Esq., b Dobbie ...	0	c Hayter b Wood	...	0
G. Bird, Esq., c Hayter b Dobbie	4	c Colvin b Dobbie	...	4
C. H. Clark, Esq., c Ainslie b Wood ..	34			
M. Marshall, Esq., b Wood ...	16	not out	...	12
M. Hickson, Esq., not out ...	5	not out	...	1
A. F. Cookson, Esq., run out ...	0			
E. McDonald, Esq., b Dobbie...	0			
E. Hickson, Esq., b Dobbie ...	0			
Byes 4, leg-byes 3, wide 1 ...	8			
	90			17

ANALYSIS OF THE BOWLING.

1st Innings.	Balls.	Runs.	Mdn. Overs.	Wkts.	Wides
H. H. Dobbie	93	47	5	4	0
R. Wood	70	31	5	5	0
G. H. Ainslie	15	4	1	0	0
2nd Innings.					
H. H. Dobbie	20	7	1	1	0
R. Wood	15	10	0	1	0

DISSYLLABLES *V.* THE SCHOOL.

This match was played on June 1st and the following days, and resulted in an easy victory for the Dissyllables, although they were deprived of Dobbie and Ainslie. Score :—

DISSYLLABLES.

1st Innings.		2nd Innings.	
E. L. Colebrooke b Growse ...	2	b Wood	27
A. Wilson b Growse ...	4	c Wood b Searle ...	17
N. J. Abdy b Searle ...	23	c Boscawen b Searle ...	9
W. T. B. Hayter b Davidson ...	0	b Wakefield b Searle	1
E. G. Wynyard c Cocks b Searle	21	b Wood	53
E. G. Colvin c Wood b Searle...	18	b Wood	0
J. F. Prinsep b Searle...	4	b Wood	11
A. Keightley c and b Wood ...	20	b Wood	0
L. H. Burrows not out ...	6	b Wood	1
B. Burrows b Wood ...	0	c Boscawen b Searle	0
G. D. Keightley b Wood	0	not out	0
Byes 3, leg-byes 2, wide 1 ...	6	Byes 12, leg-bye 1, wides 3...	16
	104		135

SCHOOL.

1st Innings.		2nd Innings.	
H. Davidson b Wilson ...	2	c Burrows b Abdy ...	18
H. Somers Cocks c B. Burrows b Wilson	14	c Colebrooke b Abdy	5
O. Evan-Thomas c Wynyard b Hayter	38	b Wilson	2
R. Wood l-b-w b Hayter ...	8	b Wilson	2
G. Searle b Abdy ...	8	b Abdy	24
S. F. Smith c Abdy b Keightley	7	c Abdy b Wood ...	0
E. F. Growse c Wynyard b Keightley ...	6	c and b Wilson ...	0
Ll. Evan-Thomas b Abdy ...	2	b Abdy	0
G. H. Boscawen b Abdy ...	2	b Wilson	6
H. Prance not out ...	0	c Colvin b Abdy ...	1
A. R. Stokes c Keightley b Abdy	1	not out	0
Byes 12, leg-byes 4 ...	16	Byes 4, leg-bye 1, wides 4	9
	99		67

A TO K *v.* THE REST.

This match was begun on June 7th, and resulted in a tie. Dobbie's innings of 110 is the largest of the year. Wood and Thomas both bowled very well in the second innings and saved the match. Score :—

REST.

1st Innings.		2nd Innings.	
H. Somers Cocks b Dobbie ...	2	c Abdy b Dobbie ...	21
Rev. W. Romanis b Dobbie ...	0	b Dobbie	7
R. Wood b Dobbie ...	1	b Dobbie	12
O. Evan-Thomas c (sub.) b Ainslie	2	c Abdy b Dobbie ...	28
G. Searle l-b-w b Dobbie ...	21	not out	0
S. F. Smith c Colvin b Dobbie	6	b Dobbie	7
Ll. Evan-Thomas b Dobbie ...	10	b Dobbie	1
J. F. M. Prinsep b Growse ...	31	b Dobbie	0
W. Prance b Dobbie ...	7	b Davidson	2
E. G. Wynyard not out ...	26	c (sub.) b Davidson ...	10
A. Wilson c Colebrooke b Dobbie	1	b Dobbie	16
Byes 34, leg-byes 2, wides 2	38	Byes 19, wides 2 ...	21
	145		125

A TO K.

1st Innings.		2nd Innings.	
E. L. Colebrooke b Wood ...	5	c Wood b Thomas	0
E. F. Growse b Thomas ...	1	b Wood	14
H. H. Dobbie c and b Thomas	110	b Wood	0
H. M. Davidson st Cocks b Wood	5	b Wood	5
L. H. Burrows c and b Romanis	14	not out	3
G. H. Ainslie run out ...	0	b Thomas	4
C. Keith Falconer run out ...	8	b Wood	0
G. H. Boscawen b Wood ...	12	c L. Thomas b O. Thomas ...	0
W. T. B. Hayter c Wood b Thomas	5	b Thomas	0
N. J. Abdy not out ...	5	b Wood	31
E. G. Colvin c Wood b Thomas	11	b O. Thomas	5
Byes 22, wides 4, no ball 1 ...	27	Byes	5
	203		67

A. R. Wood and O. Evan-Thomas were put into the Eleven on Friday, June 30th, and E. G. Colvin and E. Wynyard into the Second Eleven.

OLD CARTHUSIANS.

We here give the scores of two Elevens, which we were not able to insert in our last number :—

OLD CARTHUSIANS.—1st Eleven.

1st Innings.		2nd Innings.	
W. W. Drew, Esq., b Wood ...	0	c Thomas b Wood	6
Rev. G. S. Davies b Wood	16		
H. G. Jeaffreson, Esq., c Dobbie b Wood...	1	not out	7
E. G. Blomfield, Esq., b Dobbie	32	c Growse b Wood ...	0
Capt. Sams b Dobbie ...	12	b Dobbie	16
G. C. Carter, Esq., b Dobbie ...	12	not out	4
G. E. Smythe, Esq., b Dobbie	5	b Dobbie	16
T. J. Atherton, Esq., b Dobbie	5	run out	10
E. Williams, Esq., not out ...	1	b Dobbie	0
W. C. Williams, Esq., c Dobbie b Wood	0	run out	2
Rev. A. S. Mammat b Dobbie...	0	b Wood	3
Byes 13, wide 1	14	Byes 12, leg-byes 2, wides 2	16
	98		80

ANALYSIS OF THE BOWLING

1st Innings.

			Balls.	Runs.	Mdn. Overs.	Wkts.	Wides.
H. H. Dobbie	...	...	85	40	6	5	1
R. Wood ...	...	...	85	31	6	5	0
E. F. Growse	...	...	15	6	1	0	0
G. H. Ainslie	...	...	15	6	0	0	0

2nd Innings.

H. H. Dobbie	...	...	61	22	4	3	1
R. Wood ...	...	...	61	42	2	3	1

PRESENT.

E. L. Colebrooke b Blomfield ...	...	...	...	0
O. Evan-Thomas c Drew b Williams	...	...	...	58
H. H. Dobbie c Sams b Blomfield	...	...	...	23
A. W. Wilson st Smythe b Williams	...	...	...	71
N. J. Abdy c Drew b Williams ...	...	...	...	52
R. Wood c Davies b Williams	...	...	...	3
W. T. B. Hayter c Carter b Williams	...	...	...	1
E. G. Colvin b Williams	...	...	...	3
E. F. Growse c and b Williams	...	...	...	6
G. H. Ainslie not out	...	...	...	1
H. Davidson c Atherton b Williams	...	...	...	0
Byes 5, leg-byes 3, wides 3, no ball 1	...	...	12
				230

ANALYSIS OF THE BOWLING.

		Balls.	Runs.	Mdn. Overs.	Wkts.	Wides.	No Balls.
G. Blomfield, Esq.	...	125	83	4	2	2	1
E. Smythe, Esq.	...	90	38	5	0	1	0
J. Atherton, Esq.	...	50	25	0	0	0	0
G. Jeaffreson, Esq.	...	25	11	0	0	0	0
C. Williams, Esq.	...	83	53	0	8	0	0

The play of the Eleven was on the whole good, though there was no large scoring. Growse played very steadily for his 16, and Hayter made some very fine hits. The M. C. C. wickets fell very fast, both Dobbie and Wood being very much on the spot. The fielding was also decidedly good. The M. C. C. followed on, and were a good deal more successful in the second innings. F. A. Mackinnon played a capital innings for 45 not out, and our bowling got rather loose towards the end. Score:—

CHARTERHOUSE.

E. L. Colebrooke b Hunt	... ...	13
O. Evan-Thomas c and b Flanagan	...	3
H. H. Dobbie c Venables b Hunt	...	14
A. W. F. Wilson b Hunt	... ...	4
N. J. Abdy b Hunt	... ...	2
R. Wood b Flanagan	... ...	4
E. G. Colvin c Stansfield b Bailey	...	11
W. T. B. Hayter h-w b Bailey	...	16
E. F. Growse b Flanagan	... ...	16
G. H. Ainslie c Stansfield b Hunt	...	8
H. Davidson not out	... ...	6
Byes 3, leg-bye 1, wides 3	... ...	7
		104

ANALYSIS OF THE BOWLING.

	Balls.	Runs.	Mdn. Overs.	Wkts.	Wides.
Flanagan	105	45	8	3	0
Hunt	76	35	5	5	0
Bailey	20	5	1	2	2
R. G. Venables, Esq. ...	15	12	0	0	1

M. C. C.

1st Innings.		2nd Innings.	
W. Bird, Esq., c Ainslie b Dobbie	1	not out	3
L. Chater, Esq., b Dobbie ...	4	b Thomas	14
R. G. Venables, Esq., b Dobbie	3	b Wood	15
F. A. Mackinnon, Esq., c Abdy b Wood	3	not out	45
J. H. Giffard, Esq., c Colebrooke b Wood	7		
B. R. Stansfield, Esq., b Dobbie	0		
S. H. Sturges, Esq., b Dobbie	0		
T. H. Skinner, Esq., b Dobbie	0		
Flanagan b Wood	1		
Hunt b Dobbie	0		
Bailey not out	0	c and b Dobbie	2
Byes 7, wides 2	9	Byes 10, leg-bye 1, no-ball 1, wides 2	14
	28		93

ANALYSIS OF THE BOWLING.

1st Innings.

	Balls.	Runs.	Mdn. Overs.	Wkts.	Wides.
H. H. Dobbie	40	11	3	6	1
R. Wood	37	8	4	4	1

2nd Innings.

	Balls.	Runs.	Mdn. Overs.	Wkts.	Wides.
R. Wood	55	24	4	1	0
H. H. Dobbie	60	24	4	1	0
E. F. Growse	35	20	0	0	0
G. H. Ainslie	12	6	0	0	1
O. Evan-Thomas ...	10	3	0	1	1

CHARTERHOUSE v. THE BUTTERFLIES.

On Saturday, July 8th, we played the Butterflies, and received the first defeat of the season. The Butterflies went in first. The first seven wickets fell for 50, at which point the Butterfly team came to an end, and the rest of the runs were made by our substitutes; of these Thomas and Smith each played a good innings. In our innings, Colebrooke was unfortunately run out when only seven runs had been scored. Thomas and Dobbie stayed in for some time, and brought the score

up to 35, when they were caught in two successive overs off Barlow. Ten more were added to the score when Wilson and Wood were dismissed in the same way. Abdy continued to score fast, but was deserted at intervals of about seven runs by the rest, until he himself was bowled by Barlow. The innings finally closed for 80, so that we were defeated by 23 runs on the first innings. Score:—

BUTTERFLIES.

1st Innings.		2nd Innings.	
E. Hanbury, Esq., b Dobbie ...	7	not out	23
E. S. Stanhope, Esq., c Wilson b Wood	10	not out	8
C. W. L. Bulpett, Esq., c Thomas b Dobbie	0		
J. F. Miller, Esq., c Davidson b Thomas	5	c Thomas b Dobbie	7
Rev. W. F. J. Romanis b Dobbie	0	b Dobbie	18
L. Evan-Thomas (sub) not out	18	c Abdy b Dobbie	0
A. Ringrose, Esq., c Colebrooke b Wood	4		
F. Barlow, Esq., c Ainslie b Wood	15		
H. Somers Cocks (sub) c and b Wood	8		
J. P. Prinsep (sub) b Dobbie	8		
S. F. Smith (sub) st Colvin b Thomas	16		
Byes 9, leg-byes 4, wide 1 ...	14	Byes 2, leg-byes, wides 3...	7
	103		63

ANALYSIS OF THE BOWLING.

1st Innings.

	Balls.	Runs.	Mdn. Overs.	Wkts.	Wides.
H. H. Dobbie	120	30	11	4	0
R. Wood	100	50	3	4	1
O. Evan-Thomas ...	17	8	1	2	0

2nd Innings.

	Balls.	Runs.	Mdn. Overs.	Wkts.	Wides.
H. H. Dobbie	70	35	5	3	3
R. Wood	65	21	4	0	0

CHARTERHOUSE.

E. L. Colebrooke run out		3
O. Evan-Thomas c Bulpett b Barlow	...	14
H. H. Dobbie c Stanhope b Barlow	...	19
N. J. Abdy b Barlow	... ...	22
A. Wilson c Hanbury b Barlow	...	2
R. Wood c Bulpett b Barlow	...	0
E. G. Colvin c Hanbury b Barlow...	...	6
W. T. B. Hayter b Miller	... ...	7
E. F. Growse c Romanis b Barlow	...	2
G. H. Ainslie c Stanhope b Barlow	...	3
H. Davidson not out...	... ...	1
Bye 1	...	1
		80

ANALYSIS OF THE BOWLING.

	Balls.	Runs.	Mdn. Overs.	Wkts.	Wides.
C. Bulpett, Esq.	30	16	0	0	0
E. Hanbury, Esq.	55	30	1	0	0
F. Barlow, Esq.	54	20	5	8	0
J. F. Miller, Esq.	25	13	0	1	0

CHARTERHOUSE v. BROOKE HALL.

This match was played on Wednesday, July 12th. Brooke Hall had Holden and Shaw. They went in first, and were all out for 34. Dobbie's bowling proved very effective, as none of the batsmen seemed to be able to make anything of it. We then went in, and got 147. Colebrooke's innings of 31 was an excellent piece of steady play. He survived the first four wickets, and finally was caught off Holden. Abdy's

27 included some very fine hits; and Wood and Colvin both scored well. Mr. Merryweather's bowling was the most successful. In the second innings Brooke Hall made 25 runs for four wickets; but as the match could not be played out, we won on the first innings by 113 runs. Score:—

BROOKE HALL.

1st Innings.		2nd Innings.		
Rev. G. S. Davies b Wood	... 6	b Dobbie	... ...	6
G. C. Carter, Esq., b Dobbie	... 0			
C. G. Betham, Esq., b Dobbie	4	not out	... ...	8
Rev. W. F. J. Romanis b Dobbie	2	b Dobbie	...	6
T. E. Page, Esq., b Dobbie	... 0	b Dobbie	... ...	2
G. C. Tancock, Esq., c Abdy b Wood	 10	c Davidson b Wood...	...	1
J. H. Merryweather, Esq., not out	... ...			
Rev. J. Langford b Dobbie	... 0			
S. D. Titmas, Esq., c Davidson b Dobbie	 0			
Shaw, c Thomas b Wood	... 1			
Holden, b Dobbie	... 3			
Byes 7	 7	Byes 2	... ...	2
	34			25

ANALYSIS OF THE BOWLING.

1st Innings.	Balls.	Runs.	Mdn.	Overs.	Wkts.	Wides.
H. H. Dobbie	54	6	6	7		0
R. Wood	50	21	3	3		0
2nd Innings.						
H. H. Dobbie	31	7	2	3		0
R. Wood	30	12	1	1		0

CHARTERHOUSE.

E. L. Colebrooke c Langford b Holden	...	...	...	31
O. Evan-Thomas b Shaw ...	...	...		8
H. H. obbie c Holden b Shaw	...	...	...	10
A. W. Wilson c Shaw b Holden	...	...	...	3
N. J. Abdy b Merryweather	...	...	...	27
R. Wood c Page b Merryweather	...	...	...	21
E. G. Colvin c Merryweather b Betham	...	...	...	22
W. T. B. Hayter b Merryweather	...	...	...	12
E. F. Growse b Betham	...	...	...	6
G. H. Ainslie b Merryweather	...	...	...	2
H. Davidson not out	...	...	...	0
Byes 2, leg-byes 3	...	...	...	5
				147

ANALYSIS OF THE BOWLING.

	Balls.	Runs.	Mdn.	Overs.	Wkts.	Wides.
Shaw	125	60	6	2		0
Holden...	110	42	2	2		0
J. H. Merryweather, Esq.	40	30	0	4		0
C. C. Tancock, Esq. ...	20	10	0	0		0

NORTH v. SOUTH SIDE OF CHAPEL.

Begun July 8th. The South Side won by six wickets. Score:—

NORTH.

1st Innings.		2nd Innings.		
E. L. Colebrooke b O. Thomas	15	b O. Thomas	...	4
R. Wood b Ll. Thomas	... 37	run out	...	17
E. G. Wynyard b Ll. Thomas	... 5	c Wilson b Colvin	...	39
R. Hulton, Esq., run out	... 2			
W. T. B. Hayter b Ll. Thomas	3	c Ll. Thomas b O. Thomas...	5	
E. F. Growse b Ll. Thomas	... 4	c Wilson b Thomas ...		0
C. J. Cornish, Esq., c and b O. Thomas	... 0	(H. H. Dobbie) c Wilson b Colvin	...	36
L. H. Burrows b Ll. Thomas	... 3	st Abdy b Wilson	...	0
A. R. Stokes not out ...	... 3	c Ll. Thomas b Wilson	...	0
W. F. Norris b Ll. Thomas	... 0	not out	...	5
H. Macgeorge b Ll. Thomas	... 0	(G. H. Ainslie) b Colvin	...	5
Byes 12, leg-byes 2 ...	... 14	Byes 5, leg-byes 4, wides 3...		12
	86			123

SOUTH.

1st Innings.		2nd Innings.		
O. Evan-Thomas c Cornish b Wood ...	... ...	1	b Wood	 1
H. Somers Cocks c and b Stokes	1	not out	 26
H. Davidson c Colebrooke b Hayter	... 6		
A. Wilson c Stokes b Wood	... 6	b Growse	... 0
N. J. Abdy c Hayter b Stokes	27	not out	 26
E. G. Colvin c Growse b Wood	14	not out (retired)	... 11
J. F. M. Prinsep b Wood	... 4		
Ll. Evan-Thomas b Stokes	... 30	run out	... 0
G. H. Boscawen not out	... 29	c Burrows b Wood ...	0
A. Keightley run out	... 2		
Byes 10, leg-byes 2, wides 3, no ball 1	16	Byes 9, leg-bye 1 ...	... 10
	136		74

CHARTERHOUSE v. WESTMINSTER.

This match commenced on Saturday, July 22nd, shortly after 10 o'clock, at Charterhouse, the Westminster Eleven having come down early so as to secure, if possible, a decisive result, instead of the unsatisfactory draw in which the last two matches have ended. Charterhouse won the toss, and wisely determined to go in, Evan-Thomas and Colebrooke facing the bowling of C. Fox and Hicks. Fox bowled the first over—a maiden,—but Evan-Thomas was clean bowled by Hicks' first ball, the same bowler quickly despatching Colebrooke also; two wickets going down for 1 run. Dobbie and Colvin then came together, the latter hitting very well till he was bowled by a "yorker" from Fox; Abdy, who followed, was caught off a bumpy ball, without adding to the score, Dobbie alone being able to stand up to the bowling with any success. His 16 was a very steady contribution, including a good fiver. The rest of the innings was uneventful; Wilson hit a sixer (two of them from an overthrow), and was then cleaned bowled by Fox, while Ainslie played very well for 11, not out; the innings concluding for 60, a much smaller score than was anticipated. The pitch certainly did not play well; but the batting was undeniably weak, Dobbie and Ainslie alone showing any style. At 11.45 Westminster began with Abernethy and Ryde, and the wickets began to fall with great speed before Dobbie's bowling. C. Fox played in a most determined manner, until he was bowled by Dobbie, after making 18 in first-rate form; his batting was decidedly the best shown in the first innings of either side. Nine wickets fell for 50, leaving 11 runs for the last two men to get in order to pass the Charterhouse score. This they succeeded in doing, one or two loose balls of Wood's getting severely punished, while Benbow was certainly aided by luck. Byes, of which there were 10, formed a large item in the score; but we are only surprised that their number was not greater, owing to the roughness of the ground and the swiftness of the bowling. The fielding was very good, a great improvement on former years. The innings was over at 1, so that there seemed to be time for Charterhouse still to win the match, and to make up for their small score in their first attempt. The innings began with Colebrooke and Evan-Thomas, both of whom showed very good form. Evan-Thomas played steadily, and hit very well, promising to develope into a good bat. Colebrooke was run out off a good hit in attempting an impossible run, but his batting was very praiseworthy, his cutting being especially good. Abdy was bowled after contributing 5, but he was undoubtedly worth more runs, as also was Dobbie, in whose 9 was a very good drive. Colvin and Wood now got together, and defied every change of bowling. The bowlers seemed to be getting wide, and advantage was taken of every loose ball, till the bell rang for lunch, with the score at over 100 for four wickets. After lunch, C. Fox began to bowl rather slower, and Wood punished his first over unmercifully, hitting two 4's and a 2 to leg, while Colvin steadily increased his score, playing in very pretty style. Wood was finally given out l-b-w, his 31 being obtained by free hitting. Hayter followed, and the ball soon travelled all over the ground, his 27 comprising a 6, three 5's, and one 4. One or two chances were missed out in the long field off C. Fox, otherwise the fielding was up to the mark. Wilson also hit very well for his 16, though the batting now showed less care than it had done at the beginning of the innings, which finally closed at 5.10 for 221, Ainslie again playing well for 24. Ainslie's batting in both innings deserves great praise, being wonderfully improved since last year. An hour and three quarters now remained in which to secure the downfall of the Westminster wickets, if possible, and that it did not appear to all a necessary result in the time was shown by impatient shouts of "play," after the ten minutes' interval had elapsed. Very soon, however, all fear as to the result vanished. Three wickets fell in nine minutes; and when Fox was clean bowled by Wood for 5 it seemed hardly possible for Westminster to avert defeat. No comment is necessary on the remainder of the innings; the wickets fell in quick succession, and the innings finished for 22 runs before three quarters of an hour had passed. The Westminster Eleven seemed utterly disheartened, and made no stand against the straight bowling of Wood and Dobbie; Charterhouse being thus left victorious by 196 runs. This result was mainly due to the two bowlers, whose analysis speaks for itself. No catches were missed, and the fielding was clean and smart. With regard to the batting of the Charterhouse Eleven, Colvin, Wood, and Colebrooke all showed very good form, the former especially promises to be first-rate; while the fact that in the second innings 138 runs were made by new members of the Eleven, shows that the nervousness which was once so great a bar to success, has almost entirely disappeared. The Westminster Eleven, on the other hand, was in no way up to the mark of former years, C. Fox alone showing any real batting power; his batting, we are inclined to think, was the best shown in the match, though he was unlucky in the second innings. To conclude, there is no doubt that the Charterhouse Eleven of this year is infinitely better than it has been for some time, and there is no reason why it should not go on improving in the same way, provided the ground can be kept in a decent condition. It will be seen below that out of 13 matches played, Westminster have won 7, Charterhouse 4, while 2 have been drawn.

CHARTERHOUSE.

	1st Innings.		2nd Innings.	
E. L. Colebrooke b Hicks	... 1	run out	... ...	... 15
O. Evan-Thomas b Hicks	... 0	c and b Hicks		... 21
H. H. Dobbie b Hicks...	... 16	c J. Fox b C. Fox	...	... 9
E. G. Colvin b Fox	... 9	c and b Hicks		... 55
N. J. Abdy c Rogers b Fox	... 0	b J. Fox	...	... 5
R. Wood c Ryde b Hicks	... 7	l-b-w b C. Fox	...	... 31
W. T. B. Hayter c Fox b Hicks	2	b Hicks	...	... 27
A. Wilson b Fox	... 6	c J. Fox b C. Fox	...	... 16
G. H. Ainslie not out ...	... 11	run out	...	... 24
H. Davidson b Fox	... 3	run out	...	... 7
E. F. Growse b Fox	... 1	not out	...	... 0
Byes 2, leg-byes 2 ...	... 4	Byes 2, leg-byes 6, no balls 3 ...	...	... 11
	60			221

ANALYSIS OF THE BOWLING.

1st Innings.

		Balls.	Runs.	Mdn.	Overs.	Wkts.	Wides.	No Balls.
C. J. Fox	... ...	70	19	6	5	0	0	
G. A. Hicks	... ...	65	37	3	5	0	0	

2nd Innings.

		Balls.	Runs.	Mdn.	Overs.	Wkts.	Wides.	No Balls.
C. J. Fox	... ...	151	70	11	3	0	1	
G. A. Hicks	... ...	125	85	2	3	0	0	
J. R. Fox	... ...	72	41	2	1	0	2	
C. Ryde	... ...	17	13	0	0	0	0	

WESTMINSTER.

	1st Innings.		2nd Innings.	
H. Abernethy b Dobbie	... 3	b Dobbie	... ...	... 2
C. B. Ryde b Dobbie	... 1	b Wood	...	... 0
G. A. Hicks b Dobbie...	... 0	b Dobbie	...	... 3
A. M. Hemsley b Wood	... 1	b Wood	...	... 0
C. J. Fox b Dobbie	... 18	b Wood	...	... 5
B. M. H. Rogers b Wood	... 5	c Colvin b Dobbie	...	... 0
W. C. L. Aston c Colebrooke b Dobbie	... 5	st Abdy b Wood	...	... 3
J. R. Fox b Wood	... 5	not out	...	... 0
W. N. Taylœ b Wood	... 0	c Wilson b Wood	...	... 2
H. C. Benbow b Dobbie	... 6	b Wood	...	... 1
A. F. Gamble not out...	... 7	c Colebrooke b Wood	...	... 0
Byes 10, leg-byes 2 ...	... 12	Byes 3, leg-bye 1, wides 2	6	
	63			22

ANALYSIS OF THE BOWLING.

1st Innings.

		Balls.	Runs.	Mdn.	Overs.	Wkts.	Wides.	No Balls.
H. H. Dobbie ...	...	86	18	9	6	0	0	
R. Wood	... ...	85	33	6	4	0	0	

2nd Innings.

		Balls.	Runs.	Mdn.	Overs.	Wkts.	Wides.	No Balls.
H. H. Dobbie ...	...	35	8	4	3	1	0	
R. Wood	... ...	34	8	1	7	1	0	

1850.	Westminster won on the first innings by 20 runs.
1851.	Westminster won by eight wickets.
1865.	Westminster won on the first innings by 4 runs.
1866.	Charterhouse won on the first innings by 22 runs.
1867.	Westminster won on the first innings by 59 runs.
1868.	Westminster won in a single innings, with 17 runs to spare.
1869.	Charterhouse won by ten wickets.
1870.	Charterhouse won by seven wickets.
1871.	Westminster won on the first innings by 22 runs.
1872.	No match was played.
1873.	Westminster won in a single innings, with 17 runs to spare.
1874.	Drawn. Westminster 220. Charterhouse 121 for three wickets.
1875.	Drawn. Charterhouse 75. Westminster 52 for nine wickets.
1876.	Charterhouse won by 196 runs.

CHARTERHOUSE v. OLD WYKEHAMISTS.

On Saturday, July 15th, we played the Old Wykehamists, and won by 35 runs on the first innings. The Old Wykehamists went in first, and scored 66, T. J. Green being the principal contributor. Growse, who was put on to bowl towards the end, was very much on the spot, taking three wickets for two runs. Dobbie's bowling was as good as usual, but Wood's was not quite up to the mark. Our first four wickets fell for 12, when Abdy and Colvin got in together; but Colvin was bowled by Abbott, and Somers-Cocks then joined Abdy, who was caught, when the score had reached 75, for a capital innings of 39, including a six and two fives. The rest of the wickets brought the score up to 102, Somers-Cocks being not out for a good innings of 22. Cocks was playing substitute for Hayter, who was indisposed. Score:—

OLD WYKEHAMISTS.

	1st Innings.		2nd Innings.	
A. D. Sim, Esq., b Dobbie	4	b Wood	4
T. J. Green, Esq., b Dobbie	20		
J. H. Savory, Esq.,c and b Dobbie	0	b Dobbie	32
W. S. Trollope, Esq., b Dobbie	8	not out	2
S. C. Collin, Esq., b Dobbie	2		
H. G. Hollings, Esq., b Wood	1		
C. J. Abbott, Esq , c Thomas b Growse ... ... /... ...	9	b Dobbie	3
G. K. Lyon, Esq , b Growse	0	b Dobbie	0
H. F. Pollock, Esq., b Dobbie	3		
C. A. Hodgson, Esq., b Growse	7		
S. Shepherd, Esq., not out	1	b Dobbie	0
Byes 8, log-bye 2, wide 1	11	Byes 11, leg-bye 1, wide 1 ...	13
	66		54

ANALYSIS OF THE BOWLING—1st Innings.

	Balls.	Runs.	Mdn. Overs.	Wkts.	Wides.
H. H. Dobbie	60	20	4	6	1
R. Wood	40	33	0	1	0
E. F. Growse	15	2	2	3	0
2nd Innings.					
H. H. Dobbie	40	9	3	4	1
E. F. Growse	15	28	0	0	0
R. Wood	25	10	3	1	0

CHARTERHOUSE.

E. L. Colebrooke c Trollope b Shepherd	... ...	0
O. Evan-Thomas c Abbott b Trollope ...	...	9
H. H. Dobbie c Lyon b Shepherd	...	0
R. Wood c and b Shepherd	...	0
N. J. Abdy c Shepherd b Sim	...	39
E. G. Colvin b Abbott	...	21
H. Somers Cocks not out	...	22
A. W. Wilson b Trollope	...	3
H. Davidson c Savory b Trollope	...	2
E. F. Growse b Trollope	...	3
G. H. Ainslie b Trollope	...	0
Bye 1, leg-bye 1	...	2
		101

ANALYSIS OF THE BOWLING.

	Balls.	Runs.	Mdn. Overs.	Wkts.	Wides.
W. S. Trollope, Esq.	73	27	6	5	0
S. Shepherd, Esq	55	32	0	3	0
C. J. Abbott, Esq	45	18	4	1	0
A. D. Sim, Esq.	60	23	3	1	0

OLD CHARTERHOUSE v NEW.

This match was played on July 22nd and following days, and resulted in a victory for New by three wickets. Score:—

OLD CHARTERHOUSE.

	1st Innings.		2nd Innings.	
A. Wilson b Wood	...	3	b Ainslie	8
E. M. Short c Hayter b Ainslie	10	(C. G. Paget, Esq.) not out	27
H. H. Dobbie b Wood ...	...	5	b Thomas	15
C. A. Reeve b Growse ...	...	6	b Wood	4
N. J. Abdy c Davidson b Wood	40	c Growse b Wood ...	17
F. F. Daldy b Wood ...	...	2	(W. G. Ponsonby) b Thomas	0
W. R. Page b Wood	...	1	(H. Southwell) b Wood	8
A. T. Roberts b Wood	...	0	c Thomas b Wood ...	3
A. H. Tod b Davidson ...	...	11	b Wood	1
E. W. Bishop not out ...	...	3	b Thomas	0
R. M. Ilderton b Davidson	...	0	c and b Wood	0
Byes 9, log-bye 1, wide 1	...	11	Byes 14, leg-bye 1, wide 1 ...	16
		92		99

NEW CHARTERHOUSE.

	1st Innings.		2nd Innings.	
E. L. Colebrooke b Dobbie	...	14	b Dobbie	9
O. Evan-Thomas b Dobbie	...	2	c Bishop b Wilson ...	0
R. Wood c Bishop b Wilson	...	1	b Dobbie	23
E. G. Wynyard b Dobbie	...	0	c Southwell b Wilson	2
H. Davidson b Dobbie ..	...	2	c Reeve b Dobbie ...	0
W. T. B. Hayter not out	...	8	b Dobbie	11
E. F. Growse l-b-w b Dobbie	...	1	not out	45
E. G. Colvin b Wilson ...	...	14	not out	6
H. Somers-Cocks c and b Wilson	2		
S. F. Smith c Abdy b Wilson...	2		
G. H. Ainslie b Dobbie	...	0	run out	9
Byes 12, leg-bye 1, wides 4 ...	17	Byes 20, leg-byes 3, wides 2	25
	63		130

CHARTERHOUSE v. WELLINGTON.

This match took place on Wednesday, July 26th, and resulted in a victory for us by 47 runs on the first innings. The match began soon after 10 o'clock, Wellington going in first. Wood disposed of the first two wickets with his first two balls for no runs, and the next four wickets fell for 14. Here a short stand was made by Stafford and Acton, until the former was bowled by a very good ball from Wood when the score had reached 23. Acton was bowled soon after by Dobbie, and the ninth wicket fell for 39. C. R. Haines and Campbell made a stand at the last, the latter hitting very well, and brought the score up to 54, when Haines was caught by Dobbie. Both Dobbie and Wood bowled very well this innings, and the fielding was very good. Colebrooke and Evan-Thomas went in first for us; the latter was bowled by Kennedy in the second over, and Dobbie, who followed him, did not survive long. Two wickets had fallen for 5 runs, when Colvin joined Colebrooke. The score reached 26 before the former was caught for 14, including a fine leg hit for 6. Abdy followed, and added 20 to the score before he was got out. Colebrooke was run out soon after, and the seventh wicket fell for 65. Wilson played a good innings for 18, and Growse played well for his 9, not out. In the second innings, Wellington picked up a good deal. The first four wickets fell for 31, when Kennedy and Arnot brought up the score to 57, both playing very well. The next two wickets added 16, after which Campbell and Acton brought the score up to 99, when they both fell to Wood. Wellington was deprived of the services of C. R. Haines through indisposition. In this innings our bowling fell off considerably, except Wood's, which suffered a good deal from the ground. The fielding also got loose towards the end. In our second innings, Evan-Thomas was caught in the second over. Dobbie and Colebrooke ran the score up to 32, when the former was caught for a capital innings of 26. The next six wickets fell for 43, at which point the stumps were drawn. Ten runs were required to win, with 2 wickets to fall. In this innings, most of the Eleven seemed to have quite lost themselves. Colebrooke's innings was an excellent piece of steady play, and, with Dobbie's, may be said to have saved the match. Score :

WELLINGTON.

1st Innings.			2nd Innings.			
R. W. Arnot, Esq., b Wood	...	0	c Growse b Wood	...	...	20
O. A. Bannatine, Esq., b Dobbie		5	c Thomas b Wood	...	...	14
M. Kennedy, Esq., b Wood	...	0	c Dobbie b Wood	...	...	20
C. W. Milman, Esq., b Dobbie		7	c and b Dobbie	...	...	0
M. Power, Esq., c and b Dobbie		0	st Colvin b Growse	...	...	1
H. L. Stafford, Esq., b Wood...		5	b Dobbie	...	...	4
C. H. Golightly, Esq., c Dobbie b Wood	...	1	b Wood	...	...	4
A. F. Acton, Esq., c and b Dobbie		5	c Dobbie b Wood	...	...	15
A. L. Campbell, Esq., not out...		21	l-b-w b Wood...	...	...	15
H. A. Haines, Esq., b Wood	...	5	not out	...	...	0
C. R. Haines, Esq., c Thomas b Dobbie	...	0				
Byes 3, leg-byes 2	...	5	Byes 3, leg-byes 2, wide 1			6
		54				99

ANALYSIS OF THE BOWLING.

1st Innings.

				Balls.	Runs.	Mdn. Overs.	Wkts.	Wides.
H. H. Dobbie	...	...	...	68	24	5	6	0
R. Wood	...	...	...	55	17	6	4	0
E. F. Growse	...	...	...	10	8	0	0	0

2nd Innings.

				Balls.	Runs.	Mdn. Overs.	Wkts.	Wides.
H. H. Dobbie	...	...	...	90	26	9	2	1
R. Wood	...	...	...	107	40	4	6	0
E. F. Growse	...	...	...	20	16	0	1	0
G. H. Ainslie	...	...	...	10	11	0	0	0

CHARTERHOUSE.

1st Innings.			2nd Innings.			
E. L. Colebrooke run out	...	19	not out	...	...	9
O. Evan-Thomas b Kennedy	...	0	c and b Kennedy	...	...	0
H. H. Dobbie c Kennedy b Acton		3	c Golightly b Kennedy		...	26
E. G. Colvin c C. R. Haines b Acton...	...	...	14	b Haines	...	...	1
N. J. Abdy c Bannatine b Kennedy	...	...	20	b Haines	...	...	0
R. Wood c Bannatine b Kennedy		0	c Power b Haines	...	...	2
W. T. B. Hayter st Power b Haines	...	...	0	c Acton b Haines	...	...	0
A. Wilson b Kennedy...	...	18	c and b Haines	...	...	4
G. H. Ainslie b Kennedy	...	3	not-out	...	...	1
H. Davidson b Kennedy	...	6				
E. F. Growse not out	...	9	b Acton	...	...	0
Byes 7, leg-bye 1, wide 1	...	9				
		101				43

ANALYSIS OF THE BOWLING.

1st Innings.

			Balls.	Runs.	Mdn. Overs.	Wkts.	Wides.
A. F. Acton, Esq.	...	...	85	30	4	2	0
M. Kennedy, Esq.	...	...	71	22	5	6	1
H. A. Haines, Esq.	...	...	55	36	3	1	0

2nd Innings.

			Balls.	Runs.	Mdn. Overs.	Wkts.	Wides.
A. F. Acton, Esq.	...	...	70	18	6	1	0
M. Kennedy, Esq.	...	...	40	16	5	1	0
H. A. Haines, Esq.	...	...	30	9	2	6	0

Charterhouse v. Northbrook.

This match was played on Wednesday, August 9th, the last day of the Quarter, at Northbrook, 12 a side, and, as will be seen from the subjoined score, ended in a defeat for Charterhouse. Mr. Cattley won the toss, and elected to go in. This innings lasted for nearly three hours, but during that time only 78 runs were scored, of which Messrs. A. C. Cattley and White made most, scoring respectively 15 and 22. Charterhouse began batting with Colebrooke and Evan-Thomas, but the latter quickly retired; in fact, with the exception of Colebrooke, who played a good innings of 18, nobody made any resistance to the bowling of Woodthorpe until Ainslie came in, and then it seemed as if the runs would be pulled off, but he succumbed also, after making 15 in good style, and the innings terminated for 64. Charterhouse succeeded in getting rid of their opponents for 64 in the second innings, in which A. C. Cattley again distinguished himself by making 21. Charterhouse had succeeded in making 45 for five wickets, out of which Hayter hit 19, when time was called; consequently Northbrook won on the first innings by 14 runs. Many thanks are due to Mr. Cattley for the kind way in which he treated his opponents, and for the pleasant day they spent. The batting of Charterhouse was not at all up to the mark, and the fielding was at times very loose. Score:—

Northbrook.

1st Innings.		2nd Innings.	
Rev. A. Simmonds b Dobbie ...	0	c Davidson b Wood	11
A. C. Cattley, Esq., c Dobbie b Wood	15	b Dobbie	21
J. K. White, Esq., b Dobbie ...	22	c Thomas b Dobbie	9
M. W. Marshall, Esq., b Dobbie	0	b Wood	3
H. J. Cattley, Esq., b Dobbie...	13	b Wood	4
S. W. Cattley, Esq., b Wood ...	4	b Wood	2
W. Cattley, Esq., b Wood ...	0	c and b Wood	5
B. Marshall, Esq., not out ...	14	b Dobbie	2
G. Woodthorpe, Esq., b Dobbie	0	c Colebrooke b Dobbie ...	5
C. B. Godman, Esq., b Wood ...	1	b Wood	2
B. Cattley, Esq., b Dobbie ...	0	not out	0
O. A. Bannatine, Esq., b Wood	1	c Growse b Dobbie	0
Byes 4, leg-bye 1, wides 3 ...	8	Byes	0
	78		64

Charterhouse.

1st Innings.		2nd Innings.	
E. L. Colebrooke c M. Marshall b C. Cattley	18		
O. Evan-Thomas b Woodthorpe	1		
H. H. Dobbie b Woodthorpe ...	1	st S. Cattley b M. Marshall	2
E. G. Colvin c Simmonds b Woodthorpe	2	not out	15
N. J. Abdy c B. Marshall b C. Cattley	6	b Marshall	0
R. Wood b Woodthorpe ...	0		
A. W. Wilson c Simmonds b Woodthorpe	0	l-b-w b M. Marshall... ...	2
W. T. B. Hayter b Woodthorpe	2	b M. Marshall	19
E. G. Wynyard b Woodthorpe	0	st S. Cattley b B. Cattley ...	1
G. H. Ainslie b C. Cattley ...	15	not out	3
E. F. Growse b Woodthorpe ...	9		
H. Davidson not out	2		
Byes 3, leg-byes 2, wides 3	8	Byes	3
	64		45

Batting Averages, 1876.

	Innings.	Runs.	Largest score in one innings.	Largest score in a match.	Times not out.	Average.
H. H. Dobbie ...	22	218	26	30	1	$10\frac{8}{21}$
N. J. Abdy	22	263	52	52	0	$11\frac{21}{22}$
A. W. Wilson ...	22	263	71	71	0	$11\frac{21}{22}$
E. F. Growse ...	18	73	16	16	2	$4\frac{9}{16}$
W. T. B. Hayter..	21	148	27	29	1	$7\frac{2}{5}$
E. L. Colebrooke	21	207	44	47	1	$10\frac{7}{20}$
A. R. Wood	21	158	31	38	3	$8\frac{7}{9}$
O. Evan-Thomas..	17	153	58	58	2	$10\frac{1}{5}$
E. G. Colvin	19	216	55	64	1	12
G. H. Ainslie......	20	130	24	35	6	$9\frac{2}{7}$
H. Davidson	17	67	13	15	8	$7\frac{4}{9}$

Bowling Analysis, 1876.

	Total balls.	Total runs.	Total maiden overs.	Total wickets.	Total wide balls.	Total no balls.	Average
H. H. Dobbie ...	1957	604	161	115	13	0	$5\frac{43}{115}$
R. Wood.	1689	674	104	95	8	0	$7\frac{11}{95}$
G. H. Ainslie ...	232	84	17	5	2	1	$17\frac{2}{5}$
E. F. Growse ...	140	89	5	5	0	9	$17\frac{4}{5}$
O. Evan-Thomas..	27	11	1	3	1	0	4

The First Eleven consisted, at the end of last quarter, of H. H. Dobbie (captain), N. J. Abdy *, A. W. Wilson*, E. F. Growse, W. T. B. Hayter, E. L. Colebrooke, R. Wood*, O. Evan-Thomas, E. G. Colvin, G. H. Ainslie, H. Davidson.

The Second Eleven were: H. Somers Cocks (captain), E. G. Wynyard, L. Evan-Thomas, S. F. Smith, G. H. Boscawen, J. F. M. Prinsep, L. H. Burrows*.

CHARTERHOUSE SCHOOL.

H. H. Dobbie, a truly efficient captain, and an excellent all-round player; our unusual number of victories during the past year are mainly due to his splendid fast bowling; he fields his own bowling very cleverly; is a safe catch, and a good bat, with great hitting powers. N. J. Abdy, Treas., is very steady, and one of our best bats; has a grand defence, which, combined with fair hitting powers, has been very useful in many matches; he took to wicket-keeping rather late in the season, and with a certain amount of success, considering what little practice he had. A. W. Wilson, Sec., is sometimes a most serviceable bat, though somewhat unsteady; hits remarkably hard, and has made during the season several capital scores; is a very safe field, and brilliant catch. E. F. Growse, has been singularly unfortunate throughout the year; his style, however, is good, but he wants confidence in himself; his bowling is sometimes good. W. T. B. Hayter, a really excellent long-stop, and safe catch; he possesses immense hitting powers, which have on occasions proved most serviceable, but he has been very unlucky throughout the season. E. L. Colebrooke, is the steadiest player in our eleven; defends his wickets in a wonderfully steady manner, and is very useful for breaking the bowling; can hit very well to leg, and has seldom failed to score; always goes in first; should take care of his fielding. R. Wood, a very scientific left-handed bowler; his bowling, together with Dobbie's, has brought us safely out of many dangers; his batting, too, has often been of the greatest service to the eleven, and we shall deeply feel his loss next year. O. Evan Thomas, hits well, and his style is good, but wants stronger defence; he has nevertheless sometimes scored largely, and should be very useful next season; a brilliant field at point. E. G. Colvin, has the highest batting average; scarcely ever fails to score, and sometimes scores largely, and hits well; can keep wicket fairly, but his other fielding requires great attention. G. H. Ainslie, his batting on several occasions was useful, and on all those occasions when it was most needed; fields and throws in well; his bowling hardly comes up to what was expected from his performances last year. H. Davidson, can make runs only when he goes in last, and is then tolerably safe for a few; has good style, but is not steady enough; should pay more attention to his fielding.

BATTING AVERAGES.

		Innings.	Times not out.	Runs.	Most in an Inns.	Most in a Match.	Aver.
H. H. Dobbie	· · · · · ·	22	1	218	26	30	10·8
N. J. Abdy	· · · · · ·	22	0	263	52	52	11·21
A. W. Wilson	· · · · · ·	22	0	263	71	71	11·21
E. F. Growse	· · · · · ·	18	2	73	16	16	4·9
W. T. B. Hayter	· · · · · ·	21	1	148	27	29	7·2
E. L. Colebrooke	· · · · · ·	21	1	207	44	47	10·7
R. Wood	· · · · · ·	21	3	158	31	38	8·7
O. Evan Thomas	· · · · · ·	17	2	153	58	58	10·1
E. G. Colvin	· · · · · ·	19	1	216	55	64	12·0
G. H. Ainslie	· · · · · ·	20	6	130	24	35	9·2
H. Davidson	· · · · · ·	17	8	67	13	15	7·4

The History of Birkenhead Park

Birkenhead Park was opened on April 5th 1847 by Lord Morpeth, and had been designed by Sir Joseph Paxton, a local landscape gardener, for a fee of £800. It was an immediate success as it attracted over 10,000 visitors on its first day. Since then the park has evolved and matured though it still remains much the same as when it was first designed and laid out.

The park was the first publicly-funded park to be opened in England and was influential on a number of subsequent projects including, most notably, New York's Central Park. It was built as a result of population growth that had begun on the Wirral around that time and the realisation of the importance of providing open spaces for people in industrialised areas for their well-being and health.

Initially 185 acres of land was purchased from the estate of a Mr B. E. Price of which 125 were set aside for the park with the remaining 60 being used to build houses around the outside of the park. The money raised from the sale of the houses was used to recoup the money used to purchase the land and also build the houses and park.

Paxton's idea was to create a countryside landscape of meadows and woodland belts. The lakes are shaped to appear as sinuous rivers with views across them to features such as the Boathouse and Swiss Bridge. He also incorporated surrounding land into the park and provided a separate perimeter road for traffic, which allowed the park interior to be enjoyed by pedestrians.

In 1850 F.L. Olmsted, an American, visited the park and later became famous as the designer of Central Park, New York, into which he put many of the features he saw in Birkenhead Park. In 1977 the park was designated a Conservation Area and in 1995 declared a Grade 1 Listed Landscape by English Heritage.

Organised sports have always been an important part of the park. Birkenhead Park Cricket Club was officially started in 1846, a year before the park was opened, and the park now has two cricket clubs, tennis courts, bowling greens, and football pitches.

Birkenhead Park Cricket Pavilion

A bar and entertainment area have been added on the right-hand side and new cricket nets are now located under the white umbrellas at its rear. However the pavilion remains much as it was in Wood's day and is a small architectural sporting gem from the era.

Birkenhead Park Cricket Pavilion

This close-up shows the club's formation year displayed on high, and the ornate arch over the solid wooden door which leads into the pavilion. Perhaps it is not the original door, but Wood would have passed under the arch many times in his career with the club. The large clock is a thoughtful addition to the building's front elevation.

Inside the Pavilion

On the back wall of the pavilion is a framed list of all the century scorers throughout the club's history. Wood's 190 against Orton in 1884 is clearly visible on the left side.

Birkenhead Park Cricket Ground

And this is the view of the ground now from the pavilion, which is probably very similar to that which he would have seen as he left the pavilion to go out to bat.

Local and County Cricket

Where Reg Wood went immediately after school is not clear although from the surviving scorebooks of Birkenhead Cricket Club we find that he played for them against Liverpool in 1877. Although he failed to score in two visits to the crease, he took 6 wickets in the opposition's first-innings score of 181.

Birkenhead Park Cricket Club was formed in 1846 and was an exclusive club, with all the members having been to top public schools such as Charterhouse and Uppingham. The present clubhouse was built in 1849 so if he could return, Wood would still be able to recognise some of his old sporting surroundings. Park played M.C.C. at Lord's, Surrey at The Oval, six matches against the famous All England Eleven, and Lancashire's first match was against them.

He played against Rossall Rangers in 1878 and scored 43 not out and by the following year, aged 19, he was a regular for the Park club. England's Sandford Schultz also played for the club and was in the same eleven as Wood on several occasions.

Scores and Biographies (page 283 of Volume 16) shows Wood playing for Fourteen Gentlemen of Liverpool against United North of England between July 31st - August 2nd 1879 at Sefton Park. He dismissed George Ulyett in the first-innings as A. G. Steel bagged eight wickets. In the second-innings Wood took five wickets which included R.G. Barlow and Tom Armitage and he scored 17 and 0. The match was for the benefit of the Seamen's Orphanage.

In 1880 as well as many appearances for Birkenhead Park he went on public school tours but played for Liverpool Cricket Club. On this tour he played against Marlborough, Clifton College and Cheltenham College and took a superb tally of 30 wickets in the three matches. He toured again with Liverpool C.C. in 1881 and 1883 and on both tours returned huge tallies of wickets.

The same year, aged twenty, he had already debuted for Lancashire against Kent at Old Trafford and top-scored with 32 not out, when he came in to bat at number eight. It was to be his only first-class match that season and was under the captaincy of A. N. Hornby and the county won 6, lost 4 of their 13 matches.

Lancashire v Kent June 10th - 12th 1880.

There is no mention in *Wisden* of Wood's debut in the match report although it does comment "there was nothing remarkable in the batting throughout this match but the bowling of Watson, as good as it had been when opposed to the batting of Surrey, was marvellously successful in this context."

At the close of the first day Lancashire had been dismissed for 157 and Kent had reached 78-1. Reginald batted at number eight and ended undefeated on 32. The visitors collapsed early on the second day for 112, whereupon Lancashire made 144 in their second innings and Kent were then dismissed for a paltry 53 to lose by 135 runs. Reginald's second visit to the crease was ended quickly when he was stumped by Henty off the bowling of Bray for a single. He bowled 23 overs for 23 runs and took one wicket, that of opener the Hon. Ivo Bligh whom he caught and bowled for 15. His figures in the first innings were: 23-11-23-1, but he did not bowl in the second innings.

As he played in only one of Lancashire's matches this season his records are only annotated in the pages allocated to the county in *Wisden*.

The 1881 census shows Wood residing at the family home, but only as a twenty-one-year-old and unmarried. He played three times for Lancashire this year and top scored again with 50 in the match against Nottinghamshire and posted 52 against Surrey in mid-June. However after three appearances he did not play again for the Red Rose county until 1884, although *Lillywhite* described him in the meantime as "a really good and useful player, but unfortunately has not the time to render the county much service."

Wisden reports "Champion of the counties in 1881! A title most justly earned by a series of brilliant successes almost unparalleled in the history of County Cricket. Undefeated by a single county Lancashire won no less than six matches by an innings, with plenty of runs to spare, one by 10 wickets, one by 8 wickets, one by 216 runs and one by 50 runs and as to the three drawn games there was not the remotest chance of either of them ending in defeat, had they been played out."

After extolling the skills of Hornby and Steel, *Wisden* comments "How useful Mr Wood proved in the five innings played by him." This brief mention appears to be his first in Wisden and one of very few references to him in this famous annual.

Lancashire v Nottinghamshire June 2nd - 3rd 1881.

His first match of the season was Lancashire's second in the campaign and came at Old Trafford in the match against Nottinghamshire, although the visitors fielded seven substitutes for their better players. *Wisden* reports that "Mr Wood played admirably for his 50, giving an easy chance, however, in the latter part of his innings. He and Briggs put on 61 runs whilst they were associated."

Lancashire posted 239 but within the last one and a half hours Nottinghamshire were dismissed for just 67 (Watson and Nash getting 5 wickets apiece as the only bowlers used) after which play ceased for the day. On the second day the visitors followed on and made 175. Wood bowled three overs for 10 as first change, but.

the wickets went to Watson with 6 and Barlow with 3, Butler being run-out for 13. Lancashire was left needing 4 to win and Wood, originally down at number seven on the card and Taylor listed at number three opened the innings. Taylor failed to score; Wood managed a single and with 4 byes conceded Lancashire won by 10 wickets.

Lancashire v Cambridge University June 13th - 14th 1881.

Wisden reports "this match will be remarkable for several reasons. It was the opening match for the splendid new ground of the Liverpool Club at Aigburth. It was the match in which the Lancashire eleven suffered their one defeat in 1881; the only match in 1881 in which they had to follow their innings, and the match in which the lowest number were totalled for an innings by the county team in 1881."

Wisden also pointed out that A.G. Steel played for the opposition (he scored 11 and 9 not out and took 1-22 and 5-69) and University bowler Napier strained his right arm muscle early on having recorded figures of 6-4-20-0 and did not bowl again.

The University eleven scored 187 and Wood bowled tail-ender Wilson for 2 and then Briggs caught Napier off his bowling for 10 and he returned figures of 10-5-9-2. Lancashire were bundled out for 71 with Wood at six being dismissed without scoring, caught and bowled by Steel. Lancashire then followed on and made 153 and he scored 9 before being run-out. The University then scored 38 to win although Watson did take three wickets before the match concluded at 5.25pm on the second day, the visitors winning by seven wickets. Wood did not get to bowl in the second innings.

Lancashire v Surrey June 16th - 18th 1881.

He played in Lancashire's next match at Old Trafford and *Wisden* reports that "As neither Mr Lucas, Mr Shuter or Mr Lindsay played for Surrey, the team was rather weak but Lancashire, except for the absence of Mr Steel, played at full strength. Rain prevented a start being made until 12.40, but the wet in no way interfered with the batting for the Lancastrians who, when stumps were drawn at 5.15pm in consequence of heavy and continuous rain, had amassed 226 for the loss of half the wickets, every man in the team having got into double figures."

The next day Lancashire were dismissed for 324. Watson at number nine was top scorer with 60 not out and Wood at number six, joint second top scorer with 52, caught by Wingfield off the bowling of Potter. *Wisden* concludes *"Surrey's reply was the very poor total of 69"* – Watson and Nash bowled unchanged to dismiss them in 95 overs with Watson returning figures of 48-31-30-6 and Nash

47.1-29-37-4. At the close of the second day, Surrey were 36-1, but the hosts needed just two hours the following day to win as Surrey fell for 130. Wood held a catch off Nash to dismiss J.M. Read for 14 and bowled 2 overs for 4 runs, and this was his last match for Lancashire this year, despite the season still being in its infancy.

Wisden makes no mention of his absence for the match against Yorkshire at Sheffield which began on July 4th. The match, for the record, opened in *"glorious cricket weather"* but was later to be wrecked by rain on the third day, although Lancashire won by 50 runs.

Lillywhite had made mention of his not playing much cricket, and having ceased playing so early this year we must consider that he had a secure or decent job which he was not going to sacrifice in order to seek a career as a county cricketer.

At the close of the season Wood was third in the batting averages behind Steel and Hornby. He was unbeaten in one of his five innings, recorded a top score of 50, scored 112 runs in all and concluded the season with an average of 28.

As mentioned in the introduction, the local *Birkenhead News* is held in the British Library Newspaper Library at Colindale, London but the years 1878-1881 are in such a fragile condition as to be currently unavailable for the public to view. This is a shame as these years would no doubt contain more information about him, details of the years before his debut for Lancashire when aged 20 and perhaps some domestic details too. It may also have given us a clue as to whether he played much local cricket in 1876 and 1877.

The 1882 season in the locality began on May 6th, the principal fixture being Birkenhead Park versus Manchester which saw "capital play" by Wood, who scored 26 in their total of 135 and took four wickets as Manchester were dismissed for 104. The match was played in Birkenhead Park itself. Club records tell that Wood missed the first half of the season although no reason is given. Although he managed this appearance in early May, there is no mention of him in the local newspaper until a report in the August 19th edition on the Preston v Birkenhead Park match. As opener he scored 33 out of 84, took four wickets and held a catch as Preston were dismissed for 63. Preston's R.P. Woodhouse was out "hit wicket" but in these days this was not credited to the bowler and Birkenhead Park were a player short, Neilsen being shown as "absent". In the following match, against Northern batting at number ten, Wood scored 2 not out in his team's poor 87 all out but took four wickets as they lost by one run. However this was a second-team match. At the conclusion of the season there are unfortunately no end-of-season averages shown in the newspaper, although both match reports improve quite noticeably after this year and end-of-season averages are also included.

In 1882 Lancashire were champions again and in county versus county games both they and Nottinghamshire lost just one match each. Nottinghamshire had beaten them in one of the matches between the two teams by 37 runs and over the whole season Lancashire had lost four matches to Nottinghamshire's two. In the Lancashire section of *Wisden* no mention is made of Wood, although in fairness he did not play a match for the county this season.

Birkenhead Park's opening match for the 1883 season was on Friday, May 11th against Sefton and continued on Saturday. Wood scored 65 in a total of 181 according to the match report although he is shown as scoring just 4 in the scores displayed and Sefton replied with 106 for 3 to force a draw. Wood took all three wickets and the match was described as being watched by "a large number of spectators" in a "bitterly cold wind." He was missing from his team's eleven the following week but appeared the week after and scored 41 as Birkenhead Park beat New Brighton by 136 runs in a match played on Monday and Tuesday. The June 2nd newspaper reports on their next match, played on the Isle of Man against Castleton, and reports that Wood played "a flukey innings" of 61 and took 4 for 58 in "a humiliation", although perhaps this is journalistic licence as his team lost by 45 runs! Come the end of the month on June 30th, the newspaper reports that "we are not aware that the Birkenhead Park first eleven has played any matches since we last wrote. At any rate no report of one has reached our office."

In 1883 Hornby is still captain and Lancashire begin with seven consecutive wins, yet from the next eight matches lost five and saw Notts credited as being champions. Again there is no mention of Wood in *Wisden*, although, like last season he did not play for the county.

From newspaper reports and letters to the newspaper it appears that the previously strong Birkenhead Park club had fallen in ability recently and mention was made of their immense power in the local area in recent seasons. The cricket report on August 11th states: "The Birkenhead Park will probably soon cease to be recognised as a first-class club. Its failure to keep engagements with Manchester last Friday and Saturday will afford …." Although current seasons end in late September this was not the case in Victorian times as the September 8th report states that "the cricket seen for 1883 has all but ended" and mentions "frightful weather with which we were afflicted last Saturday."

The following week the newspaper reports that "Birkenhead Park could only make 96 against the feeble Northern, but fortunately that paltry total sufficed." Brief mention is also made of the return Egremont v Liverpool match at Aigburth today (September 15th) and the fact that Liverpool "will be assisted by R. Wood, Birkenhead Park."

The local team's averages for the season are displayed in the September 29th edition. Wood played 21 matches for the first eleven and had 23 innings, scored

547 runs, with a top score of 65 and an average of 23.18 with no not-outs. Again there were no bowling averages given for the season.

And so on to 1884, when on April 26th the newspaper makes reference to the Birkenhead Park club and wishes "to see it regain its old position as one of the strongest all-round clubs in the North of England. There is no reason why it should not do so, for it has the best piece of ground in the neighbourhood and a very influential membership roll." It went on to ask "why should it not arrange to bring the Australians to Birkenhead?" and also stated …"it might enclose its ground so that the thousands of persons who desired to see a really first-class match might be made to pay admission money before doing so". Two weeks later it mentions "R. Wood who last year was one of the greatest mainstays of his team both in the bowling and batting departments."

Birkenhead Park's first match report for the 1884 season related to a home fixture against Rock Ferry which was scheduled for two days but ended up being played over just a single day. Wood opened and scored 39 not out as his eleven totalled 86 for 2 to pass Rock Ferry's 43, and the match report shows "a win for the home club by 43 runs and 8 wickets." The following week without Wood they slumped to 41 all out against Southport Alexandria at the Lancashire seaside resort.

At county level A. N. Hornby's reign as captain continues and *Wisden* reports "the season's results as a whole do not appear in a very favourable light, as out of the eleven victories eight were scored against the weak counties of Derbyshire, Somersetshire, Leicestershire and Cheshire who were each twice defeated." More illuminating is "the most noteworthy event in connection with Lancashire cricket was the refusal on the part of Notts to play the usual out and home matches with the county Palatine on the ground that the latter employed bowlers whose delivery was unfair." Crossland for one had come to notice in past matches. This season saw Nottinghamshire as the accepted champions again.

The May 24th *Birkenhead News* reports on the match against Sefton played on a Friday and Saturday and mentions that "Great praise is due to R. Wood for the able manner in which he captained the team, as his men at all times appeared to be exactly where they were wanted." Under his guidance his team won on the first innings by 106 runs, apparently to the astonishment of the many Sefton fans present. Birkenhead Park were an improving eleven now that "its downward movement has been arrested if not altogether stopped" and in their next match, against Wigan, despite being run out for 11 in their total of 228 Wood took two wickets in the visitors' first innings of 83. The report on the next match versus Notts Castle tells that Reginald "who, by the way, has of late shown considerable ability as a wicket-keeper again distinguished himself … he played his innings of 59." Clearly his team were on the up and boosted no doubt by his qualities as a leader.

Liverpool and District v Australians June 23rd - 24th 1884.

In June, commenting on the Liverpool and District v Australians match at Aigburth, the *Birkenhead News* states that "Birkenhead was represented by its leading local cricketer, R. Wood of Birkenhead Park in the match Liverpool and District v Australians. The compliment was accentuated by Wood being put on to bowl in both innings – his trundling bowling was scarcely perhaps up to the international competition level, but he was anything but a failure."

The home team comprised: R.G. Barlow, D.Q. Steel, A.G. Steel, G.R. Cox, J. Briggs, H. B. Steel, A. Watson, H. Leach, A. Price, R. Wood and J. Crossland. Four of these would, by the end of their careers, have played for England and only Cox would not have turned out for Lancashire. Indeed, this match was his only ever first-class appearance.

The home team won the toss and elected to bat and although D. Q. Steel was removed without scoring, Barlow and A.G. Steel put on 66 for the second wicket. Steel went on to score 72, 35 more than Price's next-best score. Boyle's 5 for 33 caused the middle-order and tail to fold without offering much resistance and only Leach, undefeated on 22, offered any further cheer. Wood, at number ten was caught by Palmer off the bowling of Boyle for a single and the innings closed at 213 in 105 overs.

Crossland and Wood opened the bowling and the former dismissed McDonnell for 11 when caught by H.B. Steel. Bannerman was dismissed for 23 and Giffen for 36 and at the close of the first day the Australians were 103-5. With Crossland taking 5 for 50 to tear the middle order out and no other member of the eleven exceeding 20, the tourists were dismissed for 140. Wood returned creditable figures of 10-6-17-1.

The second innings was a disaster for the home team. D.Q. Steel again failed to score and although Barlow managed to reach 9, wickets then fell alarmingly at the other end to leave them reeling at 18 for 7. A.G. Steel was at the other end whilst this carnage was unfolding and despite his 29 and a brave 7 not-out by Wood they were routed for just 54 in 40 overs with the visitors using just Palmer and Boyle to inflict the damage. They took 5 wickets each.

The tourists then set about getting the 128 required for victory but quickly found themselves at 0 for 2 as Crossland removed Bonnor and McDonnell. Bannerman and Giffen then raised the score to 22 but both fell in quick succession, again to Crossland, and when he then removed Palmer without scoring he had plunged them to 23 for 5. Murdoch and Blackham then set about restoring some creditability to their innings and they took the score to 92 before Wood trapped Blackham leg-before for 28. The score inched up to 112 and then Wood bowled Scott for 14 and then he dismissed Spofforth with the help of Barlow for 3 to leave the tourists at 120 for 8. Crossland then bowled Midwinter for 1 which left the tourists at 124 for 9 and still requiring 4 runs for victory. Although last man Boyle failed to score Murdoch was undefeated on 38 and the tourists won a tense match by one wicket. Wood returned the impressive figures of 10-5-19-3 and had taken the wickets of Blackham, Scott and Spofforth, although these were outshone by Crossland's return of 23.1-17-20-6.

The following week (July 5th) the newspaper reports that "R. Wood has been selected to play on behalf of the Gentlemen of Liverpool and District against the Philadelphians at Aigburth next week. We wish him better luck than he had against the Australians on the same ground." The following week when discussing his failure in the above match when he "spooned the ball up", the paper reported "these collapses are very unfortunate for his reputation and they will, if repeated, prevent him from taking the national position which occasional displays in the Park would seem to warrant him in doing. Already his many admirers are induced to discount his merits."

Gentlemen of Liverpool v Gentlemen of Philadelphia July 7th - 8th 1884.

The home side was made up of: R.G. Dunlop, E. Roper, R. Wood, E.E. Steel, H.B. Steel, G. Bird, E.C. Hornby, H.B. Parr, G.F. Hornby, W.H. Potter and E. Manson. Most of these players had played for Lancashire by the end of their career, although G.F. Hornby's only first-class match was for Oxford University against M.C.C. at Lord's in 1882 when he scored 0 and 1 and took 0-35 as his side lost by an innings and 3 runs. Dunlop and Manson however never made a first-class appearance.

The Gentlemen of Philadelphia scored 185 in their first innings in this non-first-class, two-day fixture and Wood took 3 for 49 having opened the bowling. He batted at number three and was caught for 11 and saw his team dismissed for 169. Again he opened the bowling in the second innings and returned figures of 4-35 (he took the first four wickets to fall) as the Americans were dismissed for 102. He batted at number three and scored 13 which was the third-top score and although the fall of wickets details have been lost the first seven batsmen scored just 31 runs. Rearguard action by Parr and Potter took the total to a tantalising 114, but the home team still lost by 4 runs.

He did not play in the match against Cheshire at Manchester on June 30th and July 1st but played his sole game for the county eleven this season in the next one against Yorkshire on July 14th and 15th which was billed as "Allen Hill's match."

Yorkshire v Lancashire July 14th - 15th 1884

This Roses match was played at Sheffield. Yorkshire scored 128 in their first innings and Wood opened the bowling and returned figures of 11-3-26-1. He dismissed Hon. M.B. Hawke for 0, the catch being held by Barlow. Lancashire then made 170 and Wood batted at number eight but failed to trouble the scorers, being bowled by Peate. The home team were then shot out for just 72, with Wood catching Bates off Barlow, although he did not get to bowl. Lancashire then made 31 to win by 6 wickets but not before the early dismissal of Hornby for 1, Barlow for 0, Lancashire for 5 and Briggs for 4 had no doubt caused alarm.

Wisden reports "Yorkshire batted first and the only noteworthy features of the innings were the patient defensive cricket of Hall and the brilliant batting of Bates." Lancashire were 105-4 at the close of play on the first day. *Wisden* continues "the bowling was very destructive when the game was continued on Tuesday, 30 wickets going down for only 68 runs. Peate that morning took 4 more wickets for only 15 runs … Yorkshire went in again 42 runs to the bad, and made so sensational a start that at the luncheon interval half of the wickets were actually down for 15 runs." The short report which again omits any mention of Wood concludes with "It is to be regretted for the sake of Allen Hill that the match did not extend well into the third day, but as some 6,000 paid gate on the opening day, and no rain fell until about five o'clock on the second it is hoped that Hill realized a handsome sum."

Lancashire's next match was versus Surrey at Aigburth on July 17th and 18th but the match report in *Wisden* makes no mention of Wood's absence.

Lancashire v Gloucestershire July 24th- 25th 1884.

Wood's last match for Lancashire was at Old Trafford and W.G. Grace featured in the opposition's eleven. The visitors won the toss and elected to bat but soon found themselves at 38 for 5, with Barlow and Watson removing the first five and only E.M. Grace with 12 offering any show of resistance. W.G. and Brain then took the score to 90 before the latter was bowled by Watson and when Page was bowled by Barlow for 7 the West Countrymen were 107-7. W.G. was eventually bowled by Barlow for 53 and the innings closed after 86 overs for 119. Wood had not been called to turn his arm.

W.G. opened the bowling and promptly dismissed Barlow without scoring and then Hornby and Taylor took the score to 57 before the latter was caught by W.G. off Woof's bowling. Briggs scored 13 but was dismissed with the total on 79 and then two more wickets fell with the total the same including opener Hornby for 46. Wood and Robinson then took the score to 98 before the latter was dismissed for 9 and with Whittaker's 11, Watson's 9 and Wood's stubborn 22 the score was taken to 142 for 9. Crossland was dismissed before opening his account so the total remained at 142 and the home team were 23 runs ahead. Woof had been the choice bowler with 4 for 48.

Gloucestershire began their second innings and at 17 lost E.M. Grace for 14 but their innings closed on 25 for 1 before the close, so one must assume that the last day's play was rained off completely. Wood was not called on to bowl in the match and held no catches either.

Having played for four different elevens in such a short space of time, one feels safe to say that Wood clearly had a reputation as a good cricketer in his early twenties which carried on from impressive performances at his school.

Match reports continue throughout the season although again accompanying scores are often missing. He is not shown playing against Oxton in the drawn match on July 21st and 22nd (a Monday and Tuesday fixture), perhaps as he would be playing for Lancashire against Gloucestershire at Old Trafford which began on July 24th. However the three-day match saw play only on its first two days. He was allegedly present on July 25th and 26th (a Friday and Saturday fixture) for Birkenhead Park against Rock Ferry which saw its second day rained off with Rock Ferry on 93-3, having taken two of the wickets to fall. Clearly there is an error in the dates here as he is shown in two places on the July 25th!

Although later dismissed for 0 and 5 in the next match, against Dingle the paper comments "it seems a thousand pities that such fine cricketers as F.H. Pickworth, Dr. Aspinal, R. Wood and Smith (no initials given) should be lost to the Cheshire county team. No team can be truly representative that does not include these men." A couple of weeks later Cheshire's honorary secretary Mr J. Horner wrote to the paper to explain that Wood had played for Lancashire against Yorkshire "which according to the laws of cricket debarred him from playing for Cheshire this year at all events". He was absent from his team to face Bromborough Pool in the August 23rd edition, a match that they narrowly won. The local paper glowingly reported that "A Birkenhead Park match without Wood is like a Gloucestershire match without Grace, and he is so scientific and earnest a player that we always regret to see a match of his club without him". The September 13th edition sees a very brief report for the last match of the season plus details of the batting for the recent Birkenhead Club and Ground v Notts Castle match played on the latter's ground. No date is given but Wood scored 5 and took three wickets as Birkenhead Club and Ground scored 170 and Notts were bowled out for 71.

In the end-of-season batting averages for the first eleven Wood is shown as having batted in 27 innings, with one not out, 753 runs, a top score of 190 and an average of 28.25. Again there are no bowling averages and they are the only local teams' averages printed in the paper.

At county level in 1885 Hornby was still the Lancashire captain, winning 13, losing 2 and drawing 3 of their 18 matches (whereas the season before they had played 20 matches and lost 7). They again saw Notts crowned as champions. The report on the county in *Wisden* covering this season opens with mention of the dispute between Nottinghamshire and Lancashire about "unfair bowling" – Crossland and Nash are mentioned and a long letter from Kent's Lord Harris on the subject is also published.

Wood's first mention in the local press for the 1885 season comes when he is shown as scoring 6 out of 76 for his side against Rock Ferry and taking two wickets in their total of 107 in the May 9th cricket report. Three weeks later there is a report on Park's match against Werneth during which Wood was stumped for 30 in a total of 204 and Werneth were dismissed for 71. The cricket reporter also wrote the following abrupt comments about Holden, Park's wicket-keeper, "who, as a wicket-keeper is a complete failure" and that Birkenhead Park Cricket Club should put an advert in a newspaper for "a wicket-keeper who will stand up to the wickets and not five yards away, accept at least one chance out of a dozen chances offered, and not miss every one, able to stump a batter when he remains beyond the crease for a couple of seconds …" And so it continued on for a few more lines in a vein of contempt for the poor chap.

In the next match, away to Wigan, poor Holden was dismissed without scoring, but did manage to hold a catch. Wood did not play; however he played against Birkenhead Victoria on a Tuesday and scored 7 as his side made 168 for 3 and took four wickets in the opposition's 130 all out. It is interesting to note that Birkenhead Victoria's Daniels was shown as "thrown out" for 0. It was also strange to see Park shown as winning by seven wickets and 51 runs.

In early July Wood scored 28 against Dingle at Birkenhead Park as his side amassed 257 and then dismissed the visitors for 52, although he took no wickets. On Monday and Tuesday June 29th and 30th, twelve from "North of Ireland" came over "to practise against the Park team" and in a match that ensued the visitors made 46. Park replied with 243, with the newspaper noting that "Reggie was bowled" but omitting to give his score, although the fall of the wicket came when the total was 66. The visitors then managed 129 second time around, leaving Park as victors by an innings and 68 runs.

The next month saw the Park v Sefton match watched by an estimated crowd of 4,000 and they saw Wood make 2 out of 151 and then take two wickets in Sefton's 198 for 5. The August 15th edition reports on the Park against Bromborough Pool on a previous Wednesday which saw Wood score 62 as opener in Park's 332 for 6 and the visitors end on 44 for 4.

He scored 6 as opener in Birkenhead Park's total of 186 on August 22nd against Rock Ferry, who replied with 68 for 6. There is a match report for the Friday August 28th match between Park and Mr H.S. Patterson's eleven although Wood is not in the team, nor is there any sign of him in their second eleven fixture against Manchester at Old Trafford on Monday, August 31st. However the paper does mention that the team did know that they would be without him and Pinkworth for this match and this is perhaps a clue to his future.

On September 5th Park played away to Southport, instead of fulfilling the match against the same opposition at their own ground. The paper goes on to report that "The Park have lost a good man 'Regy' (sic) Wood, who has, we understand, left this country to try his fortune in the Antipodes. Ever since his connection with the Park, he has been a valuable member, one who, on more than one occasion, has pulled a game out of the fire, and infused into his colleagues new life and vigour and his departure is felt on all sides to be an unfortunate matter for the club. However, there are several young and promising players who will, it is hoped, be able to fill up the breech thus caused, but all who know 'Regy' will miss his genial face and infectious hilarity in the field."

This is the *only* reference to his personality that has come to light after many hours of research on our subject. Southport were dismissed for 48, Park having earlier made 113.

The batting and bowling averages are shown on September 19th and he is seventh in both. He batted in 20 innings and was out each time and scored 418 runs with a top score of 62 and an average of 20.18. He bowled 1,006 balls, 40 maidens, conceded 519 runs and took 29 wickets at an average of 17.26. He made no appearances for the second eleven, whose averages also appear. Birkenhead Park played 34 matches, winning 14, drawing 13 and losing 7.

There is no mention in *Wisden* of Wood's decision to emigrate so he left as anonymously as he had arrived, as his county debut failed to get a mention in 1880.

We are still no nearer answering the question of how he was passing his time in these intervening years. Perhaps he was working with his father and trying to learn the ropes to a promising career as a trader? As can be deduced from these newspaper reports he had been playing a lot of cricket for Birkenhead Park and occasionally for Liverpool and District since 1882.

To Australia

Despite a move of such distance Reggie Wood was not lost to the game. Apparently after pressure from Victoria and East Melbourne captain Harry Boyle to join his club, he scored 253 runs in the 1885-86 season at 126.5, which included 122 not out against Fitzroy.

The Gippsland Mercury reported on 13th April 1886 that:

"The East Melbourne Cricket Club has gained a great addition to its strength in Mr. Reginald Wood, a young cricketer who recently arrived from the mother country. On Saturday against Fitzroy he played a grand not out innings of 122. He has now played four innings for the East Melbourne Club in the following order: - 12 v Richmond: 82 not out v Melbourne: 37 v Melbourne University: and 122 not out v Fitzroy, giving a total of 253 runs for two completed innings, or an average of 126 runs per innings. Mr. Wood is an old Charterhouse boy and was one of the best all-round cricketers in the Liverpool and Birkenhead Park clubs, and is a well-known member of the Lancashire county X1. He is a left handed batsman, and also quite a good left-arm medium pace bowler, and playing for the Liverpool Club against the last Australia X1, when the latter won by 1 wicket, he was very successful with the ball. Boyle, the East Melbourne captain, however, considers his delivery open to suspicion, although it has been passed by R. Thoms, the celebrated English (sic) umpire, and therefore will not put him on to bowl. It is not unlikely that Wood will gain a place in the Victoria X1 should he elect to remain in the colony."

There was no mention of his emigration in the 1886 *Wisden* by which time this fact was known to the cricket followers in England.

Wisden Almanac 1888 reports (on page 322) "the team taken out to Australia in the autumn of 1886 was one of the strongest that ever left England for the colonies. It consisted of Shrewsbury, Barnes, Gunn, Scotton, Flowers, Sherwin, Shaw, Barlow, Briggs, Lohmann, Read, Bates and Lillywhite. The team took part in 29 matches of which 10 were of first-class importance. Of the 10 first-class the Englishmen won 6, lost 2 and left 2 unfinished."

The first match was at Adelaide between October 30th – November 2nd against Fifteen of South Australia, which was drawn, although England fell two wickets short of recording an innings win. Other matches followed at Melbourne, Parramatta, Sydney, Goulburn, Cootamundra, Lithgow, Geelong (December 23rd and 24th), Ballarat, Bathurst, Orange, Bowral, Camden, Narrabri, Armidale, Newcastle and Singleton (February 14th and 15th).

Victoria v Shaw's X1 November 6th - 10th 1886.

Wood's first match for the State team was at the Melbourne Cricket Ground, just over a year after his arrival in Australia and coincidentally against his fellow countrymen, in what was their second match of the tour. It was a four-day match and Wood batted at number seven but was dismissed without scoring, caught Sherwin, bowled Lohmann, in his new team's total of 329. He was one of six batsmen Lohmann removed in the first innings.

In reply Shaw's team ran up 352 and Wood assisted in the run-out of Flowers, who had scored 52. He was the eighth of nine bowlers used and returned figures of 10-4-18-0.

In the second innings he again batted at seven and was dismissed for 19, again off the bowling of Lohmann, this time caught by Bates (one of a hat-trick of dismissals by this combination) in his side's total of 207-9 as the match ended in a draw. Lohmann bowled 62 four-ball overs and took 8-80. Crowds for the respective days were given as: first day - 3,500, second day -3,000, third day - 8,000 and fourth day - 600.

Victoria v South Australia February 11th- 14th 1887.

Much later in the season he played his only ever State match at the Melbourne Cricket Ground, which was a timeless match. Victoria, under the captaincy of Midwinter, won the toss and elected to bat. McShane top scored with 39 and Wood managed to remain undefeated on 11 as his side were dismissed for just 138 with Giffen taking 8 for 83 in 42 consecutive overs.

South Australia replied with 170, opener Godfrey top scored with 40 and although the home team used seven bowlers Wood was not one of them. In their second innings Victoria made 230 in 102.3 overs. Wood, batting again at number seven, was bowled by Noel for 4 runs.

With 199 the target for victory South Australia were routed for 54 in 50 overs and Victoria, with Midwinter and Morris taking five wickets apiece, did not need to call on the services of Wood. Attendances for the three days were given as 400, 100, 200 respectively.

His team-mates in the Victoria X1 for this match were: R.S. Houston, J. McIlwraith, P.G. McShane, S. Morris, W.E. Midwinter, G.H.S. Trott, P.M. Lewis, J. Worrall, W. Over and J. Phillips.

Shaw had brought twelve players only and when Billy Barnes, renowned for sinking the odd drink, hurt his hand when he threw a punch at the Australian captain Percy McDonnell, but missed and hit the wall, Wood was invited to join the England team. Apparently Barlow and Briggs, two former Lancashire county colleagues, recommended him to the tour manager. Just four days later he was in Sydney playing for Shaw's eleven against New South Wales

New South Wales v Shaw's X1 February 18th - 21st 1887.

Shrewsbury won the toss at Sydney and elected to field. Charles Bannerman and John Swift were the umpires and with Lohmann taking five wickets the home side were dismissed for 141. Although Wood was not required to bowl he did hold two catches off Lohmann which dismissed Ferris and Turner.

The visitors replied with a paltry 99, Turner having bowled batsmen two to five each for nought to send them from the safety of 49 for 1 to 62 for 5. Only opener Bates, who had watched the panic from the other end, stood firm, with 48. Wood batted at number ten and remained unbeaten on 10. Turner took 8 for 32 off 33.2 overs and bowled seven of his victims.

In their second innings the home team managed 180 in 123 overs. Moses top scored with 73 although Lohmann took 6 for 41. Wood was the last of seven bowlers to be used and only had time to bowl 8 overs for 8 runs.

With 223 being the target for victory, Shaw's eleven were dismissed for 100, Turner again being the protagonist by bowling four of his six victims. Bates again stood firm with 40, Lohmann assisted with 26 but nobody else reached double figures. Wood batted again at number ten and was third-top scorer with 9, caught and bowled by Garrett.

Again Wood's appearance is not noted in *Wisden,* who reported solely "the third and conquering match with NSW resulted disastrously for the Englishmen who, on a slow wicket, could do nothing against Turner's bowling, and were beaten by the substantial majority of 122 runs – NSW played a splendid game, and had the advantage from start to finish."

Despite this lack of preparation Wood was selected to play his first ever Test match the following week, although it has not been possible to establish how much warning he was given of this impending debut, or indeed, if he half-expected to be called up. Presumably he would have been aware of the continuing inability of Barnes to play. The last match was all he had for a warm-up prior to the Test at Sydney which began on Friday, February 25th and whose umpires were again Bannerman and Swift.

England v Australia February 25th - March 1st 1887.

This was the second Test and was a timeless match of which *Wisden* reports "The Australian team was very far indeed from a representative one, the only Victorian player on the side was Midwinter. Jones however was the only prominent Sydney man who was away. Having the best of the play all through, the Englishmen won by 71 runs, Lohmann's fine bowling in the first innings, and Barlow's batting being the main elements of success. Turner and Ferris bowled admirably for the Australians, but their exertions were not sufficient to avert defeat."

There is a far more detailed report in *Cricket* which runs to four columns of tightly typed script. Rain fell from midnight until 10 o'clock of the morning of the first day so it was decided to postpone the start due to the wicket being in "so bad a state". Lunch was taken and after another inspection it was decided to begin play.

The Australian team was made up of eight from New South Wales, one from Victoria and two from South Australia. Blackham, Palmer, Bruce, Trumble and George Giffen were asked to play, but all declined. Giffen gave the excuse of a sprained leg, Blackham and Palmer gave no reason and Trumble and Bruce said that they could not get away from business commitments. Jones was unwell so his place was taken by twelfth man Cottam.

Shrewsbury won the toss and, after much deliberation, elected to bat and at five-to-three opened the innings with Bates against the bowling of Turner and Ferris. The score crept up to 14 whereupon Bates tried to drive Trumble but "quietly played it into the hand of Ferris at mid-on." Shrewsbury shortly afterwards played a ball onto his foot, whereupon the ball then bounced back to the stumps and disturbed a bail and when Gunn was bowled by Turner the visitors were 35 for 3. Turner then repeated the feat and dismissed Read for 11 and when Lohamnn was bowled by Ferris for 2 England found themselves at 43 for 5. Turner then sent left-hander Scotton back to the pavilion without scoring when he "sent his off-stump flying" and England were in dire trouble at 50 for 6. Briggs then came in and was missed by McDonnell at slip and then cut Garrett for two fours and Ferris for another before the latter bowler removed his bail with his score 17 runs. At 73 for 7 Flowers joined Barlow and the partnership continued until the following day when the total reached 130 whereupon Flowers was caught for 37 at mid-off, off Ferris which was the innings' top-score.

The first day had seen England 128 for 7 at the close and rain had then fallen heavily from midnight until sunrise. Play eventually started at a minute past twelve and just two byes were added before Flowers' demise. *Cricket* then reports "Wood, who again played for Barnes, came next, and Barlow got lively, but in attempting a big hit was caught at mid-off from a skyer. Sherwin made 4, when Wood was out leg before, the innings closing for 151." A perhaps too brief report on the close of the innings.

Turner and Ferris, both from New South Wales, shared four wickets apiece and both bowled 60 overs or more.

The home eleven opened with Lyon and Giffen, both from South Australia, against Briggs and Lohmann. Lohmann was in good form and bowled Giffen for 2 with the total on 12, and then with the score on 15 bowled Lyons for 11. Careful play by Allen and Moses took the score to 40 before Lohmann bowled the former for 14. Captain McDonnell set about the bowling from the outset but was soon dismissed for 10 by Lohmann, who then bowled Midwinter for a single to leave the home team at 59 for 5.

The first ball of Lohmann's next over accounted for Cottam and to date all six wickets had fallen to him. Turner and Moses took the score to 82 before Flowers caught and bowled Turner for 9 and then bowled Moses for 28. With the total on 83, Lohmann bowled Garrett for a single, and Ferris fell in the same manner and the hosts were dismissed for 84, 67 runs behind. Lohmann took 8 for 35 and Flowers 2 for 9 and Wood had not been required to bowl.

Shrewsbury and Bates opened the second innings against the bowling of Ferris and Turner and after a long sequence of maidens the score had reached 6 after 15 minutes play. At 21 Turner bowled Shrewsbury for 6, and as an aside had accounted for the wicket of the England captain in his last four innings and for just 15 runs.

After some lusty blows Bates tried to repeat the treatment but missed and was bowled by Turner. Read was then stumped for 2 off the bowling of Ferris and when Gunn fell for 10 England was 59 for 4. Ferris then accounted for Lohmann for 6, bowled on what was described as "a treacherous wicket", before "Time" was called with the score at 73 for 5 and the crowd was given as "fully 8,000, the Grand Stand being well-filled with ladies, who promenaded the lawn to some fine music from the band of the permanent Artillery."

On Sunday the temperature was about 100 in the shade although a small amount of rain fell. Play resumed on Monday and it was "clear and frightfully hot, so hot that refreshments had to be taken about every half-hour." In the first twenty minutes the score had increased by only 4 runs when "the Notts man (Scotton) was clean bowled by Ferris." Briggs was next to the wicket and runs we are told came a little more freely although with his first ball Garrett bowled Briggs for 16. Flowers then joined Barlow and the two brought up the 100 and after a lot "of slow play Flowers hit Ferris to leg for 4". The score climbed to 136 before Turner bowled Flowers for 18 and Wood, before he could score, played on. Sherwin helped Barlow to increase the total to 154 when Turner sent his wicket flying.

The Australians thus needed 222 to win and opened with McDonnell and Moses against the bowling of Lohmann and Briggs. "Runs came freely. The score quickly reached 30." It was not until the score had reached 51 that the breakthrough came, when McDonnell was caught by Gunn off the bowling of Lohmann for 35. *Cricket* then tells us that "Allen came next, Moses hitting Barlow for 3, and getting in front of Lohmann hit him splendidly over the fence for 5." However when trying to hit Bates, he missed the ball and was stumped for 33 to leave his side at 86 for 2. Lyons was next in but fell without scoring, caught at cover-point, and with 9 more added Cottam was stumped off Briggs. "Giffen was bowled first ball by the Lancashire lad, and Midwinter with Allen played out time, the total being 101 for five wickets. The attendance was about 3,000."

The report continues "Lohmann received sad news by the mail just delivered, the death of his mother, and he was naturally a bit cut up, and off colour with the ball. Shrewsbury was presented with a pair of gold spectacles during the luncheon hour in remembrance of his brace of eggs secured in the match against N.S.W., so that even inability gets its reward here."

There was a thunderstorm on the Monday night but very little rain and Tuesday was fine and cool. I shall quote *Cricket* to illustrate the close of the match: "On March 1st at quarter-past twelve the English team took the field followed by Allen and Midwinter and the latter was immediately caught at the wicket, making way for Turner, who quickly rattled up 9, when he was finely caught by Briggs close to the fence from a low hard drive. Turner now fielded for Gunn, who was unwell, and caught Allen at mid-off for a well played 30. Garrett played well for 20, when he was caught at the wicket, and the innings closed for 150, leaving the Englishmen victors by 71 runs."

Thus Wood's sole Test was not very memorable for him. He scored 6 and 0, being dismissed having played-on and did not bowl or take a catch in the game. It could however be said that he hardly had a chance to shine, coming in at number ten and not being required to bowl.

Victoria v Shaw's X1 March 4th- 8th 1887.

The next match was *against* Victoria at Melbourne so in the space of three weeks he had played both for and against them with two other matches in between those two. It should be noted that this season saw him play for and against England, so he is unique in having played both for *and* against both England *and* Victoria.

The England team had arrived in Melbourne just before noon on March 3rd whereupon most went to the races to see the Australia Cup, considered by most to be second only in the colony to the Melbourne Cup. For the record, a horse from New Zealand called Nelson was beaten by a head by the champion three-year-old of Australia called Trident.

The match began in perfect weather and Wood again replaced Barnes. Midwinter won the toss and elected to bat and after an hour Victoria had posted 75 runs. The partnership was broken when Bruce attempted to drive Briggs and was caught at mid-off by Flowers and lunch was then taken. One hundred had been posted by ten-to-three and runs flowed freely from then on until McShane was caught by Briggs at cover-point for 45 with the total at 163 for 3. There followed a ten-minute refreshment interval and shortly afterwards McIlwraith was caught at point for 64 although the magazine *Cricket* reported perhaps cruelly that the batsman "will never shine as a batsman except on such perfect wickets as Adelaide and Melbourne can produce in fine weather". The home side then collapsed with Midwinter falling for 7, caught at cover-point, Morris made 4, caught at the wicket, Houston was caught at point for 2 and Worrall fell in the same manner to leave the team reeling at 215 for 8. Phillips was then caught at slip and the innings should have been closed when Cotter hit a ball back to Bates who dropped it. Cotter then skied a shot which Read lost in the sky, and took ten runs off an over bowled by Briggs. The day closed with Cotter unbeaten on 27 and Horan likewise on 23 and the score 245-9 played in front of a crowd of about 1,000.

The following day was very hot and the innings quickly came to a close when Bates bowled Cotter with the first ball of the second over. At lunch the visitors were 63 without loss, Shrewsbury on 29 and Barlow 25, yet at four o'clock it was 125 during which time Barlow had added just 15 runs. *Cricket* commented that it was "some of the most monotonous play ever seen". The partnership was broken when Barlow was adjudged leg-before. Shrewsbury completed a century, which was greeted with "hearty and prolonged applause". Read fell for 23, Gunn then came in and the score soon passed 200 and was 220 for 3 when play ended at six o'clock. *Cricket* noted that "The attendance was the poorest ever seen on a Melbourne ground when an international match was taking place on a fine Saturday, and could not have numbered more than 2,500. A great race (the Champion Stakes) took place in the afternoon, which in all probability took large numbers away."

The magazine continued "Sunday was a dreadful day – terribly hot, with a northerly wind blowing clouds of dust down the streets of Melbourne from morning till night. Monday morning, March 7th, broke hot and fine, but soon after ten ominous clouds appeared in the west, and rapidly spread over the heavens, and before noon rain began to fall and continued the whole day, no play being possible. Tuesday was a lovely day, the match was being resumed at a quarter to twelve." The wicket "was in a poor state", seven wickets fell (six to Bruce) for 63 in the morning as the tourists innings closed on 283. Due to the heat the wicket improved after a lively start and at the close the home team were 137 for 5 and this, in front of another poor crowd of about 1,000.

The match resumed on Wednesday at noon and the home side "collapsed miserably, the remaining wickets adding only 19 runs" to be all-out for 156.

After lunch the Englishmen required 119 to win. Bates and Shrewsbury opened and saw off Midwinter and Bates and the total progressed "to rise rapidly, and in spite of several (bowling) changes and the 100 appeared after eighty minutes' play." Bates had scored 76 and his partner 24. Bates then fell, caught and bowled by Worrall for 86, so Barlow came to the wicket with 8 runs required and soon the match was won by nine wickets. Wood never bowled, held no catches and scored a single at number 10, as England won well, and was also overlooked in the *Cricket* match report which concluded with: "The day was a glorious one, but not more than 600 persons visited the ground, all interest in cricket being apparently dead in Melbourne."

Wisden reports "In this match the Englishmen were seen to conspicuous advantage, accomplishing one of the very best performances of their tour. Considering that Victoria played a first innings of 245 it was indeed a big thing to win by nine wickets. Shrewsbury and Bates batted splendidly, the latter's hitting in the second innings being exceptionally good. Shrewsbury's success was the more welcome as he had been scoring badly on the slow wickets at Sydney. His 144 was one of his finest displays. Flowers and Lohmann on one side and Bruce on the other bowled exceedingly well at various stages of the match." This match marked the end of the tour for Wood and also his first-class career.

The next match, the twenty-seventh of the tour, was again at Melbourne on March 11th, 12th and 14th at the East Melbourne Club against fifteen of their own, yet Wood was absent. William Barnes was shown as "absent hurt" in the match report which perhaps we could expect following his hand injury, yet it begs the questions "Where was Wood?" and "Why was he not called into play?"

The next match, against Sandhurst, although it is shown in *Cricket* as "Eighteen of Bendigo", began the following day and again he did not play. Perhaps he was relieved, as the team left at the conclusion of the fixture against East Melbourne and did not arrive until 11pm and then had to partake of a champagne toast. The crowd numbered about 600 and the match was drawn.

The next time we hear of Wood is when he is one of the umpires for the Non-Smokers v Smokers match which was played between March 17th - 21st 1887 at the East Melbourne ground. It was made up of members of the English team and also Victorians, and the Non-Smokers ran up 803.

Cricket reports that "the match was an extraordinary one, 422 runs being made for the loss of two wickets only in 4½ hours' batting, or at the rate of about 100 an hour." Shrewsbury beat Boyle at the toss and opened with Bruce to the bowling of Palmer and Briggs and in 45 minutes 66 runs had been scored whereupon lunch was taken. On the resumption of play "the scoring became fast and furious; the bowling was frequently changed."

Bruce fell leg-before to Palmer for 131 when the score was 195 and his innings included seventeen fours and a six. Bates fell for just 4, bowled by Palmer, and Gunn replaced him. "The bowling was hit all over the field, no less than eight of the now tired Smokers having a turn. At five o'clock 300 was posted. After this runs came faster than ever, 122 made in the next hour. Shrewsbury hit Palmer for

28 in three overs and Gunn hit Scotton nearly out of sight." The score was 432 for 2 at the close but the attendance "did not number more than 500 although it was a part holiday and lovely weather."

Play started again at half-past-twelve on Friday "in charming weather, and heavy scoring marked the day's play." Lunch was taken with the score at 514 for 3, with Gunn having just been bowled by Boyle for 150. Shrewsbury's impressive scoring continued after the break before he was caught at long-off by Duffy off Briggs for 236 (524 for 4) and Barlow then followed, bowled by Palmer for 29 with the score at 575. Two Victorian players, Houston and Musgrove, then caused "a lot of trouble. The former made 57, when a very fine catch by Briggs from his own bowling got rid of him, and soon after Musgrove was stumped for 62, made by first-class cricket." The score at this stage was 686 for 7.

Worrall and Cooper then "hit the bowling all over the field and it was not until the total had passed the highest on record in a first-class match that Read bowled Worrall for a dashing 78..... Sherwin and Cooper played out time, the latter not out 40, the game standing at 792 runs for eight wickets. This score beats by 17 runs the score made by N.S.W. against Victoria at Sydney in 1882, that being the highest in first-class cricket up till the present game.... the attendance was again a very poor one, not more than 500."

The third day began at twelve-thirty and when Cooper was caught and bowled by Briggs for 46 with the score at 803 for 9, Barnes declined to bat, so the innings closed.

Cricket continued "It was now the Smokers' turn, Palmer and Maurice Read opposing the bowling of Bates and Cooper. Thirty-seven runs had been made at lunch-time. Seventy-five minutes were wasted through the teams and pavilion being photographed, with the score (803) nailed on to the pavilion door."

The Smokers were dismissed for 356, Palmer made 113 and Briggs 86 and Bates took 6 for 73. *Cricket* tells that "About 600 spectators were on the ground. A big bicycle meeting having been arranged on the Melbourne ground drew the public from cricket no doubt in large numbers. They prefer any sport to cricket in Melbourne now, when a very few years ago it was quite the contrary, and they were cricket mad."

On Monday a hot wind blew and then a thunderstorm followed so play was not possible until after lunch. "Time" was called with the score at 135 for 5. *Cricket* adds "Briggs had again played well for 54, and Scotton, in attempting to secure the ball, picked it up, and was given out for it, after playing the last ball of the match." The report concludes with "The attendance was miserable, only about 100 being present. Briggs with four wickets for 141 runs, takes 500 cigars for the best bowling analysis. Shrewsbury also gets a 2-guinea trophy and 250 cigars for his score."

The report stated that "the teams" had been photographed. There are twenty-five men in the photograph, is this twenty-two players, two umpires and a scorer? And surely it did not take seventy minutes *extra* to compile the photograph as stated? Was it the only photograph to be taken? Whatever are the answers it may be surprising to know that a copy of this very clear photograph survives. Twenty of those in it are in cricket whites, one is dressed as an umpire (most likely Jim Phillips) and the remaining four are in plain clothes. David Frith was able to name fourteen of the players but Wood seems to have slipped the net again, as despite nearly eleven years having passed since he was photographed at Charterhouse, even allowing for the physical changes that a decade can bring none in the photograph looks conclusively like him.

The team left Victoria on Tuesday March 21st by express train for Adelaide to play the final match against South Australia. *Cricket* reported that "all arrived safely except Barnes, who, in changing trains at Ballarat, fell on the line and hurt his leg rather badly, which prevented his playing in against the South Australians. A daily express train runs from Melbourne to Adelaide in eighteen hours, the sleeping-cars being magnificently fitted up for ease and comfort!"

On Saturday March 26th the team boarded the "Masilla" at Adelaide at 7pm although owing to the huge amount of cargo they did not leave port until the following morning. They arrived at King George's Sound at 2.30pm on Wednesday March 30th and nearly all of the passengers spent the day looking around the port of Albany. At midnight they set off for Colombo and the port was reached at 6am on April 10th and they disembarked for 40 hours. The boat left Colombo at 9.30pm on Tuesday and arrived in Aden a week later at 4.30pm. *Cricket* reported that "all the men are well, and will go to Plymouth or London, where they are due about May 8th."

Each player's performances are then commented on in detail in batting average order and the report concludes with "Shaw and Lillywhite need not be mentioned as they never attempted to get into form". There is one glaring omission however as yet again Wood fails to be mentioned. He is even omitted from the long report of the tour in "*Cricket*" written by "Felix", the well-known Australian cricket critic. It should come as no surprise then to note that in the end of tour averages on page 103 of the May 5th edition of *Cricket,* all are listed except Wood and the magazine even noted that "Scotton, Shrewsbury, Gunn and Sherwin also bowled."

John Arlott wrote in 1982 about the foibles of selectors: "Some, of course, were lucky. On the 1886-87 Shaw-Shrewsbury tour of Australia, that reliable Nottingham reprobate, Billy Barnes, swung a punch at Percy McDonnell, the Australian captain, missed him, hit the wall and smashed his knuckles. In this dire emergency (William Gunn both batted and umpired) the promoter desperately called on Reginald Wood, a Carthusian left-hander who had emigrated to Australia after an unexciting career (166 runs and 4 wickets) with Lancashire. He went in number ten; scored 6 and 0, did not bowl; and never graced the Test scene again. He had, though, had his game: and he turned professional in Australia. Those less fortunate, who were never capped although they deserved it, await examination."

Scores and Biographies (page 427 of Volume 15) makes mention of him at the Albert Club in Redfern, Sydney in 1889. But it is unclear how he spent his time between his appearance as an umpire at the East Melbourne Club in March 1887 and this mention, at a cricket ground many miles away and in a different State. This period out of the limelight was for two years, but he then appears to vanish from media attention for over two decades.

East Melbourne Cricket Club

The large expanse of railway which emerges from Flinders Street station now covers the area where East Melbourne Club was once situated. It was at this ground where the photograph of the Smoker v Non-Smokers teams (see overleaf) was taken and much discussion has taken place since as to whether Wood is one of the twenty-five in the photograph. If we allow for two teams of eleven, two umpires and two scorers (or did one suffice?) then there is still room for Wood to have escaped the lens. As it is, there are four men in everyday clothes along the back row, so the chances of Wood being missed are thus increased.

Non-Smokers v Smokers at East Melbourne March 17th-21st 1887

This is one of the photographs, or, perhaps the only one taken, which held up the resumption of play in the match. David Frith identified many of the 25 people as listed, and yet again we are left wondering if Wood escaped the lens.

Along the back row, standing are: Worrall, ?, Bruce, Briggs, ?, Lillywhite and ?

Seated are: Barnes, Barlow, Shrewsbury, Umpire (with hat), ? , ?, Sherwin, ?, Boyle, Flowers, ? , Read, ? and the gent standing is also unknown.

Seated at the front are: ? ,Gunn, Bates and Walters.

The following comments on the tour of Shaw and Shrewsbury are from the pen of the well-known Australian cricket critic " Felix," in the *Australasian* newspaper :—

By the "Massilia" on Saturday night our friends the Englishmen left Adelaide for the old country. I am sure we all wish them a fair wind and a clear sky, a good time on board, and a pleasant summer and lots of runs during the season which will have commenced by the time they get home. They sojourned amongst us from the end of October to the 26th March, and during that time they played 29 matches, of which they won 12, and lost only 2. There were 15 drawn games, which would in nearly every instance have been won by our visitors if time had permitted. That they are a great team everyone will admit. In my judgment they are the finest all-round team that ever visited Australia. As a fielding team they are simply perfect, the best we have ever seen in these parts. Briggs and Shrewsbury showed perfect form at cover and at point, and Sherwin kept wicket exceedingly well. Lohmann, Gunn, and Maurice Read also appeared to great advantage, no matter what position in the field they filled. In batting there was not a weak man. Sherwin, who was set down as by no means a strong batsman, came time after time just when he was wanted. A special feature of the tour was the magnificent uphill fight against and victory over the first combined team in Sydney. The combined men thought they would have it all their own way, but the Englishmen played up in grand style, and won in a manner that reflected conspicuous credit upon them.

A very regrettable circumstance in connection with the tour is that the visitors have departed without once encountering the full strength of Australia. At the New Year a representative Australian eleven would have met the Englishmen but for the M.C.C. Australian eleven. This team, which, with its full strength, failed so signally time after time in England, could not expect to do much when two or three of the best men were absent. They played three matches against the Englishmen, and lost two, and would have lost the third had it been played out. If the Englishmen had met a strong representative Australian eleven at the New Year considerable interest would have been felt in the contest. But nobody cared much to see the M.C.C. Australian eleven play, for the good reason that, as a team, they were a pronounced failure. If, instead of meeting the M.C.C. team, the Englishmen had met the full strength of Australia at the New Year, the Victorian portion of their tour would not have been the financial frost it turned out to be.

In Sydney the public rolled up very well indeed, as many as 12,000 or 14,000 persons having been present on each of four or five Saturdays. And in the country towns the Englishmen were liberally treated in the matter of terms. But for all that the visitors have not made much money. According to their own account they have done little more than clear expenses. They thoroughly enjoyed themselves during the tour. Sherwin said :—"I came out to enjoy myself, and I have done so. I like the climate—Victoria especially, and I like the free-and-easy style of the colonists. In the country towns we had a particularly pleasant time. In the evenings we would sit in verandah or balcony and sing our favourite songs and glees, and quite a crowd would gather round to listen. On one occasion after singing at a concert each of us was presented with a gold medal as a memento. Everywhere we went we were treated most hospitably, and during our travels we saw some very beautiful scenery. But the rain! I shall never forget it. It seemed to rain in every town we visited. The rain followed us round. That is what the people said, at any rate, and they thanked us for breaking up the drought, and asked us to come again when another drought occurs. At Bowral we were above our ankles in water in our tent, and cricket bags and boots were floating about in a manner that was quite novel to us. One diverting incident was when a country umpire gave Shrewsbury out instead of Maurice Read, who was actually out. Maurice was walking away, but the umpire brought him back and told Shrewsbury that he was out, not Read. The reason was that Shrewsbury's play was too slow to suit the umpire. He preferred Read's dash. We were surprised at the poor attendances in Melbourne, and it seemed to some of us that Victorians do not attend a sport in large numbers unless the sport is associated with betting and gambling. We think Turner the finest bowler in the world on a sticky wicket. He would be a great success in England, and so would young Ferris. In our minds it is a toss-up whether Spofforth in his best day was as good on a sticky wicket as Turner. Shrewsbury cannot play Turner on a sticky wicket : he breaks back too fast. Turner and Ferris on a bad wicket are a bit ahead of any bowlers we know. The Sydney men well deserved their two victories over us, but on a good fast wicket they would not be a match for us. I like Australia and Australians so well that I shall come out again if I can."

Gunn is not so favourably impressed with the climate. He says :—"You have four seasons sometimes in one day. I have been scorched in the morning, and stone-cold in the afternoon. It is not like this at home. You get splendid sunny days, but I prefer Nottingham and the banks of Trent."

Altogether the team displayed excellent all-round form. A glance at the averages shows that Shrewsbury heads the batting list in eleven-a-side matches with 34·64 for 18 innings, and in all matches with 33·65 for 36 innings. In matches against odds, Read is top with 33·71 for 21 innings. In bowling Barnes is first in eleven-a-side matches with 13·32 runs per wicket, and against odds and in all matches Briggs heads the list. Only in two instances has a hundred been scored against the visitors, namely, by Horan—117 not out, and Boyle—115. Special attention is invited to the magnificent bowling figures of Turner in the list of Australian bowling averages against the Englishmen.

The following are the batting and bowling averages of the Englishmen for all matches of the tour:—

BATTING AVERAGES.

ELEVEN-A-SIDE MATCHES.

	Inns.	Times not out.	Runs.	Aver.
A. Shrewsbury	18	4	485	34.64
W. Barnes	12	1	319	29
W. Bates	17	0	379	22.29
W. Gunn	16	1	323	21.53
R. G. Barlow	18	3	310	20.66
W. Flowers	15	2	192	14.76
M. Read	16	0	236	14.75
G. Lohmann	15	2	191	14.69
M. Sherwin	16	8	108	13.50
J. Briggs	15	0	179	11.93
W. Scotton	16	1	163	10.86

Manly Wharf

This photograph was taken about 1887-88, and is thus a view that Wood would have been very familiar with when he lived in the flats which looked out over the beach. No doubt he would also have taken the ferry to cross Sydney Harbour, as many thousands of commuters and tourists still do today.

AGAINST ODDS.

M Read	21	0	708	33.71
A. Shrewsbury	18	3	491	32.73
R. Barlow	21	2	519	27.31
W. Bates	22	3	486	25.57
R. Barnes	14	1	328	25.23
J. Briggs	23	5	453	25.16
W. Gunn	21	1	384	19.20
G. Lohmann	20	3	318	18.70
W. Scotton	19	0	246	12.94
W. Flowers	22	3	245	12.89
M. Sherwin	20	4	87	5.43

ALL MATCHES.

A. Shrewsbury	36	7	976	33 65
R. Barnes	26	2	647	28.95
M. Read	37	0	944	25.51
R. Barlow	39	5	829	24.38
W. Bates	39	3	865	24.02
W. Gunn	37	2	707	20.20
J. Briggs	38	5	682	19.15
G. Lohmann	35	5	509	16.96
W. Flowers	37	5	437	13.65
W. Scotton	35	1	409	12.02
M. Sherwin	36	12	195	8.12

BOWLING AVERAGES.

ELEVEN-A-SIDE MATCHES.

	Balls.	Mdns.	Runs.	Wkt.	Aver.
R. Barnes	1498	225	333	25	13.32
W. Flowers	1462	196	347	24	14.45
G. Lohmann	3054	362	915	59	15.50
W. Bates	1448	172	445	21	21.18
J. Briggs	2441	306	667	30	22.23
R. Barlow	1496	183	434	18	24.11
M. Read	112	13	33	1	33

AGAINST ODDS.

J. Briggs	2838	376	756	146	5.17
R. Barlow	1176	181	250	45	5.55
W. Bates	1964	227	570	86	6.62
W. Flowers	2283	315	555	76	7.30
R. Barnes	403	57	84	11	7.63
G. Lohmann	2556	308	727	91	7.98
M. Read	338	38	108	12	9
W. Gunn	76	9	36	3	12

ALL MATCHES.

J. Briggs	5279	676	1423	176	8.08
W. Flowers	3745	511	902	190	9.02
W. Bates	3412	399	1016	107	9.49
R. Barlow	2672	364	684	63	10.85
M. Read	450	53	141	13	10.84
G. Lohmann	5610	687	1642	150	10.94
R. Barnes	1901	282	417	36	11.58

Lohmann bowled 3 wides, Bates 3, Briggs 2, Barlow 1. Barnes, Barlow, and Briggs each bowled one no-ball.

Scotton, Shrewsbury, Gunn, and Sherwin also bowled

BATTING AND BOWLING AVERAGES AGAINST THE·ENGLISH TEAM.

The following are the batting and bowling averages of Australian players who have played in not less than three innings against the Englishmen:—

BATTING AVERAGES.

	Inns.	Times not out.	Runs.	Most in an Inns.	Aver.
T. Horan (V.)	4	2	199	117*	99.50
H. Moses (N.S.W.)	10	2	308	73	38.50
H. Boyle (V.)	5	0	180	115	36
J. M'Ilwraith (V.)	7	1	2'0	64	33 33
W. Bruce (V.)	8	0	229	62	28.62
A. H. Jarvis (S.A.)	8	0	227	77	28.37
C. Richardson (N.S.W.)	4	2	53	25	26.50
R. Houston (V.)	4	0	103	66	25.75
S. P. Jones (N.S.W.)	10	0	248	48	24.80
S. Morris (V.)	4	1	66	54*	22
J. M'C. Blackham (V.)	8	0	174	63	21.75
J. Phillips (V.)	4	2	43	31*	21.50
R. Allen (N.S.W.)	8	0	163	41	20.37
P. G. M'Shane (V.)	10	0	195	65	19.50
J. Lyons (S.A.)	6	0	101	43	16.83
J. W. Trumble (V.)	8	0	134	60	16.75
H. Cottam (N.S.W.)	6	1	78	29	15.60
H. Trott (V.)	6	1	76	29*	15.20
P. S. M'Donnell (N.S.W.)	10	0	147	35	14.70
G. E. Palmer (V.)	6	0	88	27	14 66
J. M'Clinchy (N.S.W.)	6	1	68	35*	13.60
A. Hannerman (N.S.W.)	8	1	93	26	13.28
T. W. Garrett (N.S.W.)	12	1	137	31	12.45
A. Waldron (S.A.)	3	0	37	22	12.38
C. J. Turner (N.S.W.)	12	2	119	27*	11.90
J. Worrall (V.)	8	0	92	31	11.50
W. Giffen (S.A.)	6	0	59	27	9.83
W. Midwinter (V.)	6	0	57	35	9.50
C. Gooden (S.A.)	4	2	19	19	9 50
A. P. Marr (N.S.W.)	4	0	36	23	9
E. Evans (N.S.W.)	6	3	24	11	8
R Stow (S.A.)	4	0	27	13	6.75
F. R. Spofforth (V.)	8	0	46	25	5.75
J. Whiting (N.S.W.)	3	0	16	11	5.33
J. Stephens (S.A.)	4	1	12	5*	4
P. Lewis (V.)	4	0	6	4	1.50
J. Ferris (N.S.W.)	9	2	10	3	1.42
F. Burton (N.S.W)	5	2	2	2*	0.66

BOWLING AVERAGES.

	Balls.	Mdns.	Runs.	Wkts.	Aver.
C. J. Turner	1717	217	424	55	7.70
T. W. Garrett	674	88	209	16	13 06
H. Boyle	212	27	66	5	13.20
J. Ferris	1471	165	529	32	16.53
E. Evans	440	68	83	5	16.60
W. Bruce	588	64	226	13	17.38
J. Lyons	537	60	175	8	21.87
J. Worrall	482	50	189	7	27
H. Trott	778	78	300	10	30
P. G. M'Shane	732	68	291	9	31.33
F. R. Spofforth	645	62	277	7	39.57
J. W. Trumble	500	61	161	4	40.25
W. Midwinter	260	36	81	2	40.50
G. E. Palmer	520	55	179	4	44.75
S. Morris	144	14	68	1	68
J. Phillips	224	29	55	—	—
S. Jones	92	7	33	—	—

A Trip Home

A few days before this book was due to be printed, and thus for the second time, publication was delayed, and for good reason. Warwick Torrens, the fount of knowledge with regard to cricket in Queensland, Australia whom I had liaised with when in Australia, got back to me to say he had found some scraps of news relating to Wood. One nugget was a quote which suggested Wood came back to England in mid-November 1907 and returned to Australia in early January 1909. Further it was stated that he had played some cricket whilst in England, although there was no indication given of the standard that he played.

This necessitated a return visit to the Newspaper Library in Colindale, London and the reliable *Birkenhead News* verified the information given by Warwick. Match reports for local cricket games begin with the May 6th 1908 edition but there is no sign of Wood appearing for any of the local sides. In their first match of the new campaign Birkenhead Park travelled to play Ormskirk and won by 50 runs.

In the May 2nd edition "Umpire" had written that he "dropped in at the home of Birkenhead Park a few days ago and found everything in apple pie order" …. and that …. "Sam Faulkner enters upon his 26th year as groundsman and as skipper Cecil Holden will guide the team through a heavy match list." He goes on to report that "Several new players have joined and these include F.A. Solomon, who did good service for New Brighton a season ago."

There is no sign of Wood playing in the locality amongst the match reports for the next month, although in the June 24th edition (on page 3) there is a small headline; "Mr Reggie Wood Home Again". The newspaper reports that "The links which were broken in the home of Birkenhead Park sporting circles by the departure many years ago of well-known players are gradually being mended. Some months ago Mr. W. Black returned from abroad, and news is to hand that Reggie Wood has arrived in Birkenhead. The Park warrior of the eighties was at the nets on Monday evening, and enjoyed a gruelling practice of nearly an hour's duration. Mr. Wood is as keen on the game as of yore, and doubtless we shall see him participating in a match in the very near future."

The newspaper also covers Birkenhead Park's home fixture against Sefton and "Umpire" reports that 10,000 people watched Park bat on the Saturday. The home team reached 195 and Sefton were then dismissed for 113. Park were in second place in the local championship and after six matches, they had won five matches and lost just one, and had ten points.

In the next edition on June 27th (page 3), there is more news about Wood when the newspaper reports "The exclusive announcement made in Wednesday's "News" that Reggie Wood (known to the popular world as "Gammy" Wood) was back in the old country and licking himself into condition for another spin at club cricket created great interest among our readers. Mr "Reggie's" great feats on behalf of the Park club in the early eighties are fresh in our memory, and his deeds will go down in the annals of Birkenhead Park when the present generation of man has passed away. We hope it will be possible to see Mr. Wood and Mr. Cecil Holden on one side before the end of the season, and it would add another page to the history of these veterans to see them opening a Park innings yet once again."

On July 1st the newspaper reports on the match against New Brighton, due to last two days and begun on a Monday evening in front of 3,000 people. Park won by 7 wickets and only needed one evening to secure a win. With this win they went top of the table with 15 points, having won seven out of their eight matches, and 6,000 people watched them defeat Bootle in their next match.

In early August, 3,000 saw them run up 325-7 against Western who were then dismissed for 113 and by now, after 13 matches Park were still top having won 9, drawn 1 and lost 3. In second place were Oxton and in third, New Brighton.

There is a small headline on page 3 of the *Birkenhead News* dated Wednesday August 19th 1908, entitled "Reginald Himself Again." The newspaper reports on the Birkenhead Park second team's fixture against Upton .... "The visit of Upton to the Park on Saturday provided a very interesting game up to a point, but in the end the Uptonians steered clear of defeat. The Parkites ran up the useful total of 195 and pressed the Uptonians to 124-8 wickets. One of the features of the contest was the re-appearance after many years of Reggie Wood, who played capital cricket for 40. Those who remembered the dashing Parkite in his best days saw much of his old cleverness in his latest effort, and the linking up of the "hero of the eighties" caused immense satisfaction." Wood now aged 48 had opened the innings and top scored with his 40 before being dismissed "bowled Alcock". Meanwhile the first eleven travelled to and beat Wigan by six wickets to stay joint top with Oxton on 19 points.

In the August 22nd newspaper (page 3) there is another small headline "Reggie Wood Redidivus" under which is another short report about the local boy now back home. "The re-appearance of Mr. Reginald Wood in a Park cricket team links up the past with the future, and revives memories of bygone days which still live in the minds of thousands of local enthusiasts. Mr. Wood's return to this district was made known through the medium of the "News" some months ago, and from the form he showed at the nets it rested with himself when he would play in a match. The old Parkite turned out against Upton and made 40 in his best style."

Four days later the newspaper reports that Park beat Huyton to go a point clear at the top of the table, and also that Wood again opened for the second team, also against Huyton, who were dismissed for 182. Although the bowling averages are not printed, he is not shown as taking any wickets or holding any catches in the opposition's innings, and in Park's reply he again top scored with 49 before being dismissed "LBW Davies". Park was dismissed for a total of 148 to lose by 32 runs.

These two second eleven appearances were sadly not a practice for the forthcoming Park versus Liverpool fixture, which was drawn. Liverpool made 218-5 and Park replied with 133-8 and there is no sign of Wood playing for another local team amongst the match reports either.

On Saturday September 2nd the newspaper reports that Park made 227-4 against Neston, who replied with 108-7 and after 16 matches Liverpool was now top with 22 points and Park second one point behind.

The following week, the cricket reports feature on the front page and Bootle make 181-5 against Park, who reply with 153-6, although there is no table shown so we are left to wonder who won the local championship as there are no tables shown in subsequent editions. The averages for Birkenhead Park and its second eleven also appear and Wood is in the "the following also batted" section under the main averages which shows scores of 40 and 49. The second eleven played 21 matches, won 5, drew 10 and lost 6 and the first eleven played 30 matches, won 19, drew 7 and lost 4, although Wood did not play any first-team cricket for them whilst in the country.

View over Manly circa 1915

A view over Manly looking towards the ocean beach. St Ronan's Hospital, at 59 North Steyne, is in the road lined with pines fronting the ocean beach. The back of the hospital is about three-quarters across the photograph from the left hand side.

This photograph is courtesy of Manly Library.

The Corso

This photograph was taken in 1915, the year Wood died. The Corso is the main street in Manly and links the Sydney Harbour beach with the ocean beach, which are separated by only a thin piece of land.

Earls Court

The block of flats called Earls Court, where Wood lived at the time of his death, has been knocked down and replaced by this small block of flats. They still give idyllic views over the beach area of Manly and out towards Sydney, on the other side of the vast harbour

Manly War Memorial

The memorial is to be found at one end of The Corso and lists the casualties around its base. Wood was dead five months and two days after the start of The Great War, and many of his town's folk would be killed in action before hostilities ceased. Next to his unmarked resting place in Manly Cemetery is a headstone to commemorate Major Angelo Talbot Hatton, a casualty of the war, although his body rests in Ypres, Belgium.

And Rugby Too

I typed up the information that I had gleaned about Wood's visit back to Birkenhead in 1908 and was about to submit it to the printers when I received a letter from Chris Elston, who lives near Birkenhead. He wrote following an article that I had written for the Association of Cricket Statisticians, called "Cricketers in Cathedrals" in which I made only a passing reference to our subject. He had written the history of the Birkenhead Cricket Club on the occasion of its 150th anniversary, but like others had not been able to find a photograph of their England star. In the book there is a photograph of the 1885 Birkenhead Park eleven and needless to say, Wood is missing.

Chris recently found a photograph of an R. Wood in a local history book, although he is in rugby colours. It is the same photograph that is to be found hanging up in the clubhouse of Birkenhead Park Rugby Club.

I mentioned this finding to Ann Wheeler, the Charterhouse archivist, who informed me that the school was not a rugby-playing school but a football one. Thus if this photograph is the second one of him to come to light, he must have found rugby to his liking after leaving school.

I returned to the Newspaper Library to establish if the local newspaper had also covered Birkenhead Park Rugby Club's matches as thoroughly as local cricket. I was also keen to establish whether the R. Wood in the photograph was definitely Reg Wood.

Many of the newspapers from this era have been deemed as "unfit for viewing" and have not yet been copied onto microfilm. However those dated 1882, 1884 and 1885 were available to view. There are hardly any rugby reports in the newspaper in 1882, but in the November 25th edition, listed under "Football" is a brief report of Birkenhead Rangers' match against Egremont. There are no Woods playing and no reports for Birkenhead Park Rugby Club.

Rugby received scant coverage in the local paper and was listed under "Football". The game we now call football was often referred to as "Association Football".

On December 2nd a Birkenhead Park association football match is reported on and a week later Birkenhead Rangers' match against Toxteth gets a full column devoted to it, but again, there are no Woods mentioned. In 1884 there was no mention of a Wood in the November 1st report of the Birkenhead Park versus Old Boys match and hardly any rugby matches are reported on this year.

There is an improvement in 1885 and on January 14th there is a large report on the Birkenhead Park v New Brighton match and the following week another long report on their match against Gymnasia, played at Sefton Park, which they won by "a try to nothing". In this latter match there is an A.G. Wood playing as a forward, who is most probably his younger brother, Alexander Galt Wood.

On January 31st no Woods feature in the report on the Liverpool v Birkenhead Park match played at St Ann's ground. But just to illuminate the amount of sport being played in the area, on February 7th there are reports on some association football matches and these feature Birkenhead against Cambrian in Stanley Park; Birkenhead Rovers, who played in Birkenhead Park; Birkenhead Argyle, who also played in the park, and Birkenhead Wanderers. There is no sign of Wood trying his luck with the round ball in any of the respective reports.

Birkenhead Park Rugby Club has kept a healthy amount of their early records as well as scrapbooks, and these tell that Reg played four times for Cheshire between 1878-82 as well. He also played in two international trial matches; for North of England against Wales in 1881 or 1882, (the club honours board shows 1881 but the club's history book states 1882) and a first such match in 1880.

The records also show that Mr Milligan, club captain between 1881-83, also had a photo of Reg Wood, dating from the 1877/78 season, although this has no doubt been lost in the passage of time. Thus, we can deduce that Reg played for Birkenhead Park within two years of returning from Charterhouse and was clearly talented at this sport too. However despite the club displaying a huge bank of team photographs from 1880, very few are from this decade, so it is impossible to establish how many seasons he played for the club. Despite this the records draw me to conclude that this photograph is indeed of our subject.

A.G. Wood played 11 times for Cheshire between 1886-92, was awarded his club colours in the 1889/90 season and was still a club member in 1921.

Birkenhead Park Rugby Club
team photo 1880

BIRKENHEAD PARK FOOTBALL CLUB,

SEASON 1880-1881.

G.COWIE   C.PHILLIPS   G.STEWART   S.B.MIDDLETON   R.WOOD   H.BRANDON   A.A.BLACK
W.P.EVANS   J.R.WILSON
ARCHIE WILLIAMSON   JOHN RAVENSCROFT   H.M.BLYTHE   D.A.BINGHAM

A.C.BLAIN   G.K.SMITH   J.B.PARRY   E.A.BEAZLEY

This photograph is currently on display inside the clubhouse and is in the top left-hand corner of what is a huge collection of team photographs through the years. Although high up and thus hard to photograph, it is possible to see that there is an R. Wood standing three in from the right on the back row. As mentioned on the opening page of the last chapter, rugby was often referred to as a football and this explains the title of this photograph being Birkenhead Park Football Club.

Enlarged Photo of Wood

This is an enlarged profile of Wood taken from the photograph on the previous page. Although it is from a different angle to the school cricket one and taken four years later, there are no startling differences in facial appearance. From the information given by the rugby club, the fact that they have kept such precise old club records and that his brother was also a long-standing member of the club, I am happy that the R. Wood shown is our subject.

Yet Missing From So Much

Wood had played just twelve first-class matches, six for Lancashire between 1880-84, one match for Liverpool and District against the touring Australians at Aigburth, Liverpool in June 1884, and two for Victoria in the 1886-87 season after emigrating to Australia, one of which was against the England team in November 1886 at Melbourne. He also played for Shaw's X1 against New South Wales in February 1887, against Australia at Sydney in the second Test in February 1887, and again in the last match of the tour, against Victoria at Melbourne in March.

He then became a professional coach shortly afterwards and joined East Melbourne in 1887-88 and then Melbourne Cricket Club in 1888-89, although by 1889 he had moved to the Albert Club in Sydney.

Towards the end of his article R.L. Arrowsmith raises an interesting question, having noted that Wood was engaged at the East Melbourne Club "and later, it is said, about 1889 with the Albert Club in Sydney. Whether he was the Wood who, on his only appearance for New South Wales in 1887-88, made 81 in a high-scoring match against Victoria in Sydney is not clear. The initials are variously given as H., J. and R.: if it was not he, then it seems to have been some totally unknown player. At any rate at this point our knowledge of his cricket career ends completely." Further research has established that this Wood was not our subject.

Charterhouse School kept tabs on their old pupils and a book that details old pupils dated September 1887 shows his address as Slatey Road, Claughton, Birkenhead, but again no number is shown. Yet by this year he had already sailed for Australia. A similar book dated September 1888 gives his address as "Melbourne Club, Australia". It does not appear that Reginald married before emigrating as there are very few with his name shown as marrying between 1876 and 1913 and most have middle names which he did not.

With so many brothers and sisters who would have married and had children themselves there must be a great number of folk still residing in the Birkenhead area who are distantly related to him and who in all probability are unaware of the star in their family tree. A letter to the current local newspaper, however, failed to flush any out who may still be living in the area.

After a promising start in life highlighted by two years at one of the country's top schools and a promising career as a cricketer, he decided to emigrate but carried on playing in the Melbourne area. Yet apart from a recorded visit home in 1908 little else has come to light about him. Chris Elston had heard that Wood only returned home once. So perhaps the 1910 visit that has been mentioned is two years out as Wood does not feature in any matches in 1910. The only snippet of information that has been gleaned after his return to Australia is that in 1911 he was employed as a sheep-farmer for McPhee and Company in Richmond, north Queensland, a huge distance from his last two places of employment in the country.

The next piece of information which relates to him is his death on January 6th 1915, on the other side of the globe. Another Charterhouse book, the publication date of which is unknown, lists old pupils apparently in the order of when they joined the school. Under "Oration Quarter" for 1874 Wood is listed in the register as "born 7th March 1860, sixth son of John Wood of Liverpool, cotton broker: Cricket X1 1876, Lancs Cricket X1 1880-4: Went to Australia: Played for England v Australia 1886-87 and professional cricketer in Australia and later a book-keeper on sheep stations in Queensland: died in St. Ronan's Hospital, Manly, NSW 6th Jan 1915". Clearly some sort of contact was kept with him.

His death did however come as England's sons realised that the promise made at the start of "The Great War" that "You'll be home for Christmas" had not materialised. Little did they know of the carnage and slaughter that would follow, which would also see the deaths of over 300 first-class cricketers.

Arrowsmith concludes his article with the following "His later life seems to have been unsuccessful and it appears unlikely that he was ever (as stated in the Charterhouse Register) a sheep farmer: doubtless he was employed on a sheep station. In 1910 he did pay a visit to his relatives in Lancashire. Latterly he was employed as a book keeper at Manley (sic) in New South Wales and on January 6th 1915 he died at St. Ronan's Hospital there and was buried in Manley General Cemetery."

Manly Cemetery is thought to be the fourth-oldest cemetery still in use in Sydney. It is one of only two major burial grounds from the 19th century on Sydney's North Shore – the other being Gore Hill Cemetery at St. Leonard's where incidentally Test players Reginald Duff and Dave Gregory are interred. Wood shares Manly Cemetery with Peter Stoneman (1816-83) "Outback pioneer transported (as a convict) in 1835", Richard Weatherstone, the longest-lived of those within the cemetery's walls, who died in 1938 aged 103, Charles David Jones Bryant, official war artist with the A.I.F. in the Great War, Tom "Rusty" Richards (1887-1935) rugby union player and the only player to represent both Australia and England, and who served at Gallipoli and also won the Military Cross in France, to go with an Olympic gold medal for rugby. Bill, his brother, who also played rugby five times for Australia, lies with him, and also in the cemetery is fellow rugby international Frank "Banger" Row (1877-1950), who captained Australia in the first rugby union Test against the British Isles in 1899. To continue the sporting theme, Oswald "Ossie" Merret, swimming coach and manager of the Australia Olympic team at the 1924 Paris Games is interred there too, as is the celebrated female Emmeline Du Far (1882-1935), the first woman to climb Mount Cook in New Zealand.

Manly Cemetery

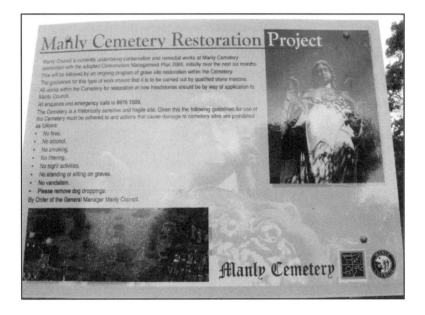

On arrival at the cemetery, I was delighted to see this sign, signifying that the local council is "currently undertaking conservation and remedial works at Manly Cemetery … initially over the next six months. This will be followed by an ongoing program of grave site restoration with the Cemetery." It was a delight to behold.

Manly Cemetery

continued

This photograph shows clearly the open style of the cemetery, and the fact that it is only surrounded by a low wooden fence. Houses around its edge are able to see right across the cemetery to the abodes on the other side.

Wood's death certificate shows his address as "Earls Court, Manly" and an advert taken from *Manly Daily* of September 14th 1907 illuminates it graphically – "Earls Court is a fashionable residential palace at Manly, and is conducted on continental principles. The points of vantage at Earls Court are: All the bedrooms are large, airy and well furnished. The linen, blankets and bedding are of the finest description that money can buy, while each bedroom has a telephone. Ladies and gentlemen's lavatories are on each floor. The guests at Earls Court have the free use of the balconies and flat roofs, from which a splendid view of the harbour and the ocean can be obtained. The restaurant is the most charming dining-room in Australia, and will seat 200 persons, private dinners or banquets being specially catered for. There is a large drawing-room and smoking-room on the first floor. Accommodation is provided for motor cars and bicycles. The boat fares (by yearly ticket) are less than tram fares to any suburb in Sydney. Earls Court is like Eden Studios – everything of the best quality at bagatelle rates."

Even allowing some leeway for "sales talk" by the owners of this prestigious block it portrays enough splendour to take one away from the assumption that he fell on hard times at the end of his life. Today the view from the block is over the point where the ferries ply their trade across the harbour between central Sydney and Manly so it afforded a spectacular view even in his era.

Reginald Wood died with no relatives nearby, and from heart failure due to poisoning of the heart from alcohol, at St. Ronan's Private Hospital, located in North Steyne, a road which fronts the ocean beach and which was very close to his last residence. The hospital closed on April 30th 1963, according to the records of the local health authority. He was buried the day after his death, an inquest being shown as "unnecessary", and at the expense of the Public Trustee, and no next of kin is given in the burial register. He was buried in plot U272 in a mixed denomination area of the cemetery, where he has lain for over ninety years, so far from his birthplace, seemingly forgotten - and worse, unmarked.

In the column on his death certificate for "Informant" of his death "no relations" has been entered and even in the column for "Where born and how long in the Australian Colony or States", "(Place: not known), England" and "not known" have been entered. The age shown on his death certificate shows him a year younger than he actually was and in the columns set aside for details of parents and any children, "not known" is recorded. The only domestic fact they felt certain to put in and of which we were unaware when we began to research his life was "unmarried."

Research was hindered greatly by his drifting out of public life or at least away from the attention of any English media between 1889 and 1908 (ages twenty-nine to forty-eight) and despite much research nothing about him has surfaced between these years. From the limited amount of knowledge we have about his jobs in Australia perhaps he was successful in these fields and also able to draw upon some of his father's finances after his death in 1887? We must also wonder when he became aware of his father's death. Was he given family money on his return to Birkenhead in 1908, or on the other hand, had he been successful enough to fund a trip home to see his relatives with ease?

With nearly all of his adult life unaccounted for we can surmise very little, but his death, unmarried and childless, of alcoholic poisoning at such a young age and with hardly anything registered about him on his death certificate, runs parallel to many who suffered a fall from grace or never escaped the poverty or despair into which they were born. However, if we take into account his final address then perhaps he did not seek any limelight in his life, was happy with his jobs and life, reasonably prosperous and enjoyed the odd drink albeit with a weak heart? Did he own his last abode? Was it rented? Or did he take a room in a friend's house? It has proved impossible to answer these questions.

Having managed to lose track of him for most of his adult life it is disappointing that having traced a few details about his last five years we cannot conclusively say how he spent these years. In health? Nomadic? Regularly drunk? Or perhaps he is destined to remain equally enigmatic in death as he was when alive?

When our hunt began for anything about his life in order to put it into one accessible place, it soon became obvious that little about him had been recorded in any cricket books. A lot of research with other agencies in Australia and England has thrown up some worthwhile and previously unknown facts but the character and personality of the man still elude us. There is surely nobody still alive who can remember meeting him although maybe somewhere in the Cheshire area there are some photographs of him in a family album for his visit home in 1908, although these would have had to survive two world wars.

Even *Wisden Almanac* contains very few details about Wood when he was alive, and on checking the publication for the years following his death he was completely overlooked. The 1916 *Wisden* runs to 298 pages and opens with some sports-related adverts between pages 4-17 in amongst which is to be found Sydney Pardon's preface on page 13. He notes the decision "to dispense with the customary photographs" and continues "owing to the limits of space I have been compelled to leave out of the births and deaths of cricketers – a valuable section of the almanac". This edition is unfortunately but understandably packed with details of war-casualties. Lord Harris's obituary of W.G. is between pages 68 and 73 and there is another write-up between pages 84-88, followed by his career statistics between pages 89-122. So about one seventh of the publication is given over to the great man. A.E. Stoddart's obituary is next between pages 123-24, Trumper's is between 131-32, Ponsonby-Fane's is between 138-39 and then the casualties the Great War inflicted on the game are listed between pages 140 and 222. The latter entries make up about a quarter of the almanac's pages.

News even reached *Wisden* (page 215) that William Wharton, who was born in Manchester, had died aged 83 in Brooklyn, New York on October 16th. He played for New York v Philadelphia at Camden and was one of the organisers for Manhattan C.C. Yet there is no mention of Wood's demise, which came at the start of the year.

In the 352-page 1917 *Wisden*, Pardon writes in his preface about those lost in war and mentions others who have died although not "killed in action" e.g. Lubbock, Penn and Horan – yet there is still no mention of Wood's death. The births and deaths of cricketers section returns and runs from page 33 to 142 yet there is no mention of him here either. "Other deaths in 1916" runs from page 237 to 267 and there are even two entries on page 267 under the sub-title "particulars of the following deaths were not received in time for inclusion in Wisdens' Almanac for 1916" – yet Wood has been overlooked or missed again.

On pages 240-41 of the 1918 *Wisden* there are listed a few deaths from 1915 and 1916 and still Wood is not accounted for, and neither is there any mention of him in the births and deaths section.

I checked various *Wisdens* at random and he does not feature in the births and deaths section in 1927, 1947, 1965 or 1972. In 1979 there was a re-classification of those who will or will no longer feature in this section. One guarantee of being included from that date was; "players who have appeared in a Test match for England", so he finally makes an appearance on page 1,072 of the 1979 Wisden Almanac - 63 years after his death. On the flip side, out went those deemed "players of no special fame or interest."

As mentioned earlier, *Scores and Biographies* makes mentions of him at the Albert Club in Redfern, Sydney in 1889 and goes onto say that he was now (in 1925) believed to be residing in Richmond, Queensland. If *Wisden* and *Scores and Biographies* were unaware of his death, then perhaps nobody in the cricket world was aware either. One must also wonder when his family became aware of his demise, and when informed, whether they in turn omitted to tell his cricket friends and contacts.

There is a small number of England capped players of whom we know very little, but for each one we have a photograph and their counties often retain some details. As Wood played only six matches for Lancashire it is not surprising they too are lacking both personal details and a photograph. Thus, as we feared at the start, he remains the least known of those capped by England, the fifty-fourth person to have been so in his case.

Despite leaving England in late August or early September 1885 to seek a new life, he was sought out by the England captain when he found himself "one short" so his whereabouts were still known a year later and his cricket ability remembered. Four years later, he was still coaching cricket, and then with no known explanation he appears to have vanished for twenty-one years.

We must therefore be thankful to Charterhouse School, who have kept much of his academic and sporting achievements and were still kept up to date about his address in Melbourne after his decision to leave England.

Charterhouse School contacted me just before this book was due to go to the printers, to say that a Mr Rob Wood, a family relative had very recently been in contact with them trying to elucidate some details about Reginald too. I contacted Rob and it transpired that he was the grand-son of one of Reginald's brothers, so Reginald was his great uncle. My hopes of any more photographs coming to light were dashed when he stated that he had no photographs of Wood. He was aware of his brief England career but in turn wanted to know if he had fathered any children.

When Mr Wood contacted me I hoped that as most people had a photograph of their grand-parents, then perhaps some may survive in the family of the brother of this grand-dad too. However it seems that Wood even escaped the camera of family members or, perhaps if a snap of him was taken, it has been lost in the passages of time.

I postponed the publication of this book again for about six months in order to get it checked thoroughly. It would thus be published after my return from Australia, which in turn would allow me to undertake some research around Sydney and also give me the chance to trace his unmarked grave and get a photograph of the plot.

As mentioned earlier he died at St. Ronan's Hospital in Manly, Sydney. On this site now stands a building called "Burradoo", which I am told is all that remains from the days of the hospital, it being part of the nurses' accommodation and ancillary buildings. A book in Manly library about the history of local suburb Warringah tells us (on page 74) when referring to hospitals in the area that "Manly Cottage Hospital being a general hospital only, twentieth century midwifery care took place in private homes or in private hospitals. Neighbours and friends gave assistance when necessary .... The first private hospital of any note was "St Ronan's" in Manly, which commenced in 1903. State Archives records indicate a bed capacity of 14 in 1919, with a licence for the care of medical, surgical and midwifery. In 1931 the bed capacity was for 16 patients, but only for medical and surgical." The population of Manly in 1890 was about 8,000 and today this number has risen to about 30,000.

In "A History of Manly-Warringah District Cricket Club 1878-1978" by Tom Spencer, there is no mention of Wood in the section listing all those players to have represented the club between these dates.

I visited the New South Wales State Library in the heart of Sydney where records of births, deaths and marriages and immigration records are kept, and for each State too. I was unable to find any assisted immigration records for Wood for Queensland. Assisted records relate to those who normally came for a job and

St Ronan's Hospital in 1925

The hospital opened in 1903 although, even in 1919 it had a bed capacity of only fourteen. This photograph shows the building, located on North Steyne, as it appeared in 1925. On the following page is a photograph taken from the same spot in 2006, although a road now appears to cut in from the right and it is hard to recognize any of the buildings.

St Ronan's Hospital in 2006

The only part of the building which still remains is the two-story one on the right of this photograph, which, I was told, was once accommodation for nurses and ancillary buildings.

NEW SOUTH WALES

REGISTRATION NUMBER

1915/ 001203

BIRTHS, DEATHS AND MARRIAGES REGISTRATION ACT 1995

DEATH CERTIFICATE

Date and place of death	Name and occupation	Sex and age	Cause of Death Duration of last illness; medical attendant; when he last saw deceased	Name and occupation of father Name and maiden surname of mother	Informant
1915 6 January St. Romano Hospital *(late of Earle's Court Manly)* MUNICIPALITY OF MANLY	Reginald Wood Book Keeper	Male 53 years	Heart Failing *(due to Senile Decay of the Heart)* No doctor (2) Inquest necessary H. P. Hawkins Coroner (3) (4) 6 January 1915	(1) Not Known (2) Not Known (3) Not Known	Certified by L. De Mazzini No relation St. Romano Hospital Manly

Particulars of registration	When and where buried; name of undertaker	Name and religion of Minister and names of witnesses of burial	Where born and how long in the Australasian Colonies or States	Place of marriage, age, and to whom	Children of marriage
(1) E. T. Ogg (2) 7 February 1915 (3) Manly	(1) 7 January 1915 (3) General Cemetery Manly Thomas Baugh	(1) A. G. Stoddart (3) Church of England E. Tierny A. B. Haines	*(About Known)* England (3) Not known Not known	(1) Not married (3) Not Known	years. 2

Before accepting copies, sight unaltered original. The original has a coloured background.

His Unmarked Grave

The photograph shows the sad sight which is his unmarked plot. Those immediately around him are marked which only adds to the tragedy, and here he has lain for over 90 years, half a globe from home and seemingly almost forgotten.

who had been sponsored or had a skill and who could thus find work. I found in the 1915 Electoral Roll for Manly a Reginald Rhodes Wood residing at 89 Darnley Road, Manly, a short distance from where he eventually died. His profession was shown as a teacher, so this may be him, or it may not be. It should be added that there was no trace of him in the area in the 1913 Electoral Roll, nor the 1909 one (which is the earliest that I could find) either. There is a microfilm record of the deaths in Manly in the official 1889-1918 New South Wales Birth, Death and Marriage records. He is listed along with 30 other Reg Woods although, his mother's details are shown as "unknown" and in the column for his father's details, it is rather strangely marked "53 years Manly".

The Earls Court block of flats where he was living at the time of his death has since been demolished and is now replaced by another block. It is located just behind an aquarium called "Oceanworld", and is thus another marker that has been erased from his life.

With few headstones numbered it took me over half an hour to trace his unmarked plot after a hilly walk of some 20 minutes from the centre of Manly. It is an unusual cemetery in that there is no stone wall around its perimeter, just a very low fence, and it therefore has a rather open feel to it, surrounded by houses which have an uninterrupted view into its centre. Coincidentally Melbourne Street leads down to the cemetery from one side.

Wood is buried next to a headstone to the memory of Major Angelo (Alf) Talbot Hatton who hailed from Newtown in New South Wales, and who died on November 9th 1917 aged just 21. Hatton's father Alf, who died on July 5th 1915 aged 49, is also marked on the headstone, but he will be on his own underneath, as Major Hatton is actually buried in Belgian Battery Corner Cemetery in Ypres, Belgium. The exact location of grave in the cemetery is unknown however, and he has one of the three "Special Memorials" amongst the 573 casualties of The Great War in this cemetery.

Wood's plot is located on the Harland Street side of the cemetery and in section "U", which is roughly central. Tragedy continues in death, as one grave to his right is that of Francis Grace aged just 15, two to the right is Jessie Brown aged 2, three to the right is Irence Luker aged 25 and whoever are four, five and six to his right are also unmarked. Seven to his right is Christopher Jackson-Inns aged 29 who died in 2002, and next to him is a memorial to Richard Charles Badmington, who died on October 14th 1918 aged 29, which is marked "died of pneumonia whilst a POW in Germany", although he is actually buried in Cologne Southern Cemetery in Germany. He resided at 22 Whistler Street, Manly which is about half a mile from the cemetery and was the son of George and Annie.

If we go the other way, then those in the graves second and third to his left are in unmarked plots, the headstone for fourth along is broken and Angus Buchanan "infant son of D+S McKinnon, aged 1 year old and 2 months – another bud in heaven" is five to his left. The next plot along is, like Wood's also unmarked.

Behind Wood's unmarked plot is a headstone for a George Robey, who died in 1941 aged 55. Many will remember an English comedian with the same name (1869-1954) who went on stage as "The Prime Minister of Mirth", and who coincidentally married Ethel Haydon from Melbourne, but the row of graves in which Wood rests is anything but humorous, more an abundance of young deaths.

To assist anybody who would like to locate his plot in the centre of the cemetery, one first needs to find the tall, black, circular, obelisk-style stone memorial to a deceased by the name of "Fuller", who died aged 55 on September 22nd 1915. From this memorial, travel one grave down (away from the playground) and then ten to the left and Wood's unmarked plot will be found next to one of the very few graves which are numbered.

He is one of a number of early England cricketers to be buried overseas – for example, the two Studd brothers (one is buried in Africa and the other in America), Thomas Armitage is interred in Chicago, Charles Absolom in Trinidad, and Jack Ferris is buried in the Church of England Section of West Street Cemetery (Grave No 54, Block 24) in Durban, South Africa. And there are several more.

As mentioned before, Reginald Wood's death certificate tells that he never married or had children, so his resting place so far from where he was born, and his death at such a young age, may add to any thoughts that we have concerning his isolation or even loneliness.

Four players have played for both Australia and England; Ferris, as mentioned above, is buried in Durban, South Africa; William Murdoch is in London's Kensal Green Cemetery; Billy Midwinter is in Melbourne General Cemetery, Australia; and Sammy Woods is buried in Taunton, Somerset. Thus, along with Midwinter, Wood is the only cricketer to have played for England to be buried in Australia (Ben Hollioake, Harold Larwood and Tony Lock were cremated) and as Reginald Wood is interred in an unmarked plot, this tale has a poignant final curtain.

Chris Elston copied brief details of many of Wood's prominent performances from the Birkenhead Park C.C. scorebook. He found details from the 1877 season, three years before his earliest mention in the local press, although perhaps due to earlier copies of the newspaper being too fragile to be viewed at The Newspaper Library. The club's scorebooks do not go back before 1878, so it is still impossible to establish when his first match for Birkenhead Park C.C. occurred.

I have copied the details below from Chris's letter and they are a pertinent addition to his early cricket career. All relate to his appearances for Birkenhead Park C.C.

1877

v Liverpool - scored 0 in both innings batting at number 11 and took 6 wickets in their first-innings total of 181

1878

v Rossall Rangers - scored 43 not out.

1879

v Childwell - scored 60 in Park's total of 130.

v Notts Castle – took 6 wickets in their first-innings total of 63 and scored 42 not out in Park's second innings.

v North Brighton - scored 55 not out in Park's total of 138 and took 7 wickets in their first-innings total of 57 and 6 in their second-innings total of 81.

v Manchester - took 5 wickets in their total of 153.

v West of Scotland - took 7 wickets in their first-innings total of 38.

v Grange (Edinburgh) - scored 40 in Park's first innings.

v Oxton - took 7 wickets in their total of 47 and then scored 42.

v Sefton - took 8 wickets in their total of 106.

v Liverpool - took 6 wickets in their total of 66.

1880

v Childwell - took 6 wickets in their total of 109.

v Dingle - took 7 wickets in their total of 136.

v Grange (Edinburgh) - took 5 wickets in their total of 162 and scored 56 in Park's total of 152.

v Sefton - took 9 wickets in their total of 181.

1881

v Childwell - took 7 wickets in their total of 99.

v Sefton - took 8 wickets in their total of 139 and scored 41 not out in Park's second innings.

v Preston - scored 54 in Park's total of 166.

v Dingle - took 8 wickets in their total of 85.

1882

v Bromborough Pool (who played with 15 in their team) - took 8 wickets in their total of 110 and it is noted that he missed the first half of the season although we cannot establish the reason.

1883

v Sefton - scored 65 in Park's total of 181.

v New Brighton - scored 41 not out in Park's total of 216-6.

v Castleton - scored 61 in Park's total of 136.

v Oxton - scored 50 in Park's total of 326-5.

v Liverpool - took 8 wickets in their total of 240.

v Northern - scored 46.

v Dingle - took 7 wickets in their total of 109.

v Incognito - took 6 wickets in their first-innings total of 96 and 5 wickets in their second-innings total of 57.

v Northern - took 6 wickets in their total of 68.

1884

v Rock Ferry - took 6 wickets in their total of 43.

v Notts Castle - scored 59 in Park's total of 201.

v Oxton - scored 190 in Park's total of 370-3 and other opener Dunlop scored 119.

v Werneth - took 5 wickets in their total of 66 and scored 52 in Park's total of 140.

v Boughton Hill (Chester) - scored 93 in Park's total of 142.

1885

v Wavertree - scored 61 in Park's total of 273.

v Wigan - scored 47 not out in Park's total of 194.

v Bromborough Pool - scored 62 not out in Park's total of 382.

v Northern - his bowling figures are given for the first time: 24-7-61-4.

v Incognito - took 7-2-17-2 with 1 wide.

v Rock Ferry (his last match, played on August 22nd) - scored 6 and his bowling figures were 4-1-19-0.

He also went on public school tours, but played for Liverpool C.C. and details of these matches follow:

1880

v Marlborough 119 and 116
24-9-53-3 and 28-11-42-7
Liverpool 286.

v Clifton College 167 and 173
41-13-66-4 and 28-6-72-6
Liverpool 185 and 158-7.

v Cheltenham College 57 and 101
17-7-24-7 and 25-6-53-3
Liverpool 172.

1881

Marlborough 132 and 121
26-12-65-6 and 32-14-48-4
Liverpool 111 and 143-8.

Clifton College 141 and 154
took 5 wickets in 2nd innings
Liverpool 85 and 197.

v Cheltenham College 99 and 142
25-8-36-4 and 42-13-81-5
Liverpool 239 and 3-0.

1883

v Marlborough 88 and 90
took 3 wickets in first innings and 6 in second innings
Liverpool 88 and 91-3.

v Cheltenham College 223 and 86
took 5 wickets in second innings
Liverpool 277 and 44-6.

The tracing of cricketers' graves and any memorials to cricket or cricketers has been a hobby of mine since 1996. I have found well in excess of a hundred England players' graves in tranquil rural churchyards, suburban cemeteries and even some abroad. I have also found just over a hundred memorials.

If any player is fortunate enough to have a cricket motif etched onto his headstone as in the case of Tom Richardson, Maurice Tate and Doug Wright, that is a bonus. But I would be happier to establish that all capped players had a headstone marking their final resting place. It is unfortunate in this respect that Wood joins Billy Brockwell, Alf Dipper, Bill Lockwood and Frank Sugg in being an England player buried in an unmarked plot.

January 6th 2015 will be the 100th anniversary of Wood's death and if the current Test match pattern is kept to, along with Australia's tradition of certain Test matches beginning on certain dates, then the scheduled last day of the Sydney Test will fall on that anniversary.

It would be a timely and apt event for the powers that be to arrange for a headstone to be unveiled over his body. The day after the Test would be acceptable, one day late over a century can be forgiven, and perhaps a member of the England party could oblige with the unveiling.

If anybody would like to start the ball rolling…

The Author

......and one of the author in Manly Cemetery, over the unmarked grave of the subject. He spent five weeks of the winter in Australia, catching up with friends, researching both this book and another on the graves of Australian Test players whilst suffering England's dire Test performances at Melbourne and Sydney. He has been a member of Surrey C.C.C. for twenty-seven years and is a member of The Cricket Society, The Cricket Memorabilia Society and The Association of Cricket Statisticians.